Coal

Other Books of Related Interest:

Opposing Viewpoints Series

Conserving the Environment

Energy Alternatives

Global Resources

Global Warming

Oil

At Issue Series

Is Global Warming a Threat?

Current Controversies Series

Alternative Energy Sources

Conserving the Environment

Pollution

"Congress shall make
no law . . . abridging
the freedom of speech,
or of the press."

First Amendment to the U.S. Constitution

The basic foundation of our democracy is the First Amendment guarantee of freedom of expression. The Opposing Viewpoints series is dedicated to the concept of this basic freedom and the idea that it is more important to practice it than to enshrine it.

Coal

Michael Logan, Book Editor

GREENHAVEN PRESS

An imprint of Thomson Gale, a part of The Thomson Corporation

Detroit • New York • San Francisco • New Haven, Conn. • Waterville, Maine • London

THOMSON
GALE

Christine Nasso, *Publisher*
Elizabeth Des Chenes, *Managing Editor*

© 2008 The Gale Group.

Star logo is a trademark and Gale and Greenhaven Press are registered trademarks used herein under license.

For more information, contact:
Greenhaven Press
27500 Drake Rd.
Farmington Hills, MI 48331-3535
Or you can visit our Internet site at http://www.gale.com

LIBRARY OF CONGRESS CATALOGING-IN-PUBLICATION DATA

Coal / Michael Logan, book editor.
    p. cm. -- Opposing Viewpoints
  Includes bibliographical references and index.
  ISBN-13: 978-0-7377-3908-4 (hardcover)
  ISBN-13: 978-0-7377-3909-1 (pbk.)
  1. Coal. 2. Power resources. 3. Coal mines and mining. I. Logan, Michael.
  TN800.C63 2007
  333.8'22--dc22
                                                                2007029810

ISBN-10: 0-7377--3908-8
ISBN-10: 0-7377-3909-6

Printed in the United States of America
10 9 8 7 6 5 4 3 2 1

Contents

Why Consider
Opposing Viewpoints?

> *"The only way in which a human being can make some approach to knowing the whole of a subject is by hearing what can be said about it by persons of every variety of opinion and studying all modes in which it can be looked at by every character of mind. No wise man ever acquired his wisdom in any mode but this."*
>
> John Stuart Mill

In our media-intensive culture it is not difficult to find differing opinions. Thousands of newspapers and magazines and dozens of radio and television talk shows resound with differing points of view. The difficulty lies in deciding which opinion to agree with and which "experts" seem the most credible. The more inundated we become with differing opinions and claims, the more essential it is to hone critical reading and thinking skills to evaluate these ideas. Opposing Viewpoints books address this problem directly by presenting stimulating debates that can be used to enhance and teach these skills. The varied opinions contained in each book examine many different aspects of a single issue. While examining these conveniently edited opposing views, readers can develop critical thinking skills such as the ability to compare and contrast authors' credibility, facts, argumentation styles, use of persuasive techniques, and other stylistic tools. In short, the Opposing Viewpoints series is an ideal way to attain the higher-level thinking and reading skills so essential in a culture of diverse and contradictory opinions.

In addition to providing a tool for critical thinking, Opposing Viewpoints books challenge readers to question their own strongly held opinions and assumptions. Most people form their opinions on the basis of upbringing, peer pressure, and personal, cultural, or professional bias. By reading carefully balanced opposing views, readers must directly confront new ideas as well as the opinions of those with whom they disagree. This is not to simplistically argue that everyone who reads opposing views will—or should—change his or her opinion. Instead, the series enhances readers' understanding of their own views by encouraging confrontation with opposing ideas. Careful examination of others' views can lead to the readers' understanding of the logical inconsistencies in their own opinions, perspective on why they hold an opinion, and the consideration of the possibility that their opinion requires further evaluation.

Evaluating Other Opinions

To ensure that this type of examination occurs, Opposing Viewpoints books present all types of opinions. Prominent spokespeople on different sides of each issue as well as well-known professionals from many disciplines challenge the reader. An additional goal of the series is to provide a forum for other, less-known, or even unpopular viewpoints. The opinion of an ordinary person who has had to make the decision to cut off life support from a terminally ill relative, for example, may be just as valuable and provide just as much insight as a medical ethicist's professional opinion. The editors have two additional purposes in including these less-known views. One, the editors encourage readers to respect others' opinions—even when not enhanced by professional credibility. It is only by reading or listening to and objectively evaluating others' ideas that one can determine whether they are worthy of consideration. Two, the inclusion of such viewpoints encourages the important critical thinking skill of objectively evaluating an author's credentials and bias. This evaluation will illuminate an author's reasons for taking a particular stance on an issue and will aid in readers' evaluation of the author's ideas.

It is our hope that these books will give readers a deeper understanding of the issues debated and an appreciation of the complexity of even seemingly simple issues when good and honest people disagree. This awareness is particularly important in a democratic society such as ours in which people enter into public debate to determine the common good. Those with whom one disagrees should not be regarded as enemies but rather as people whose views deserve careful examination and may shed light on one's own.

Thomas Jefferson once said that "difference of opinion leads to inquiry, and inquiry to truth." Jefferson, a broadly educated man, argued that "if a nation expects to be ignorant and free . . . it expects what never was and never will be." As individuals and as a nation, it is imperative that we consider the opinions of others and examine them with skill and discernment. The Opposing Viewpoints series is intended to help readers achieve this goal.

David L. Bender and Bruno Leone,
Founders

Introduction

"Coal is definitely not going away. We can plaster our country with solar cells, which aren't economic, and windmills, and everything else, and we're still not going to make a dent in our energy needs."

Andrew Perlman,
CEO of GreatPoint Energy Corporation

The nineteenth century was the age of industrial engineering. Mechanical ideas were translated into machinery that replaced human sweat and muscle. England, France, Germany, and the United States produced mechanized economies and consumer goods in previously unimagined volume and consistency. Consumer goods were transported around the globe in large quantity via ships and railroads with steam engines.

This Industrial Revolution was fueled by coal. Steel was required for building machinery. To produce one ton of iron required seven to ten tons of coal. The "dark rock" was also the main fuel for the engines that drove new machinery and transportation.

Coal has had an underestimated impact on world history. Author Barbara Freese, in her book *Coal: A Human History*, imagines a world in which coal did not push forward the Industrial Revolution:

> To grasp the magnitude of coal's global impact, we must try to picture history without the momentous, high-intensity pulse of industrialization that started in Britain and then swept the world. The mainly agrarian [farming] world would have stayed in place for decades or centuries longer, with slower technological progress, less material wealth, and more gradual social change. . . . This [is] not to suggest the world

would have been necessarily stable and peaceful, as a glance at our planet's violent preindustrial history shows. If human progress had been more dependent on harnessing surface energy rather than mineral energy [coal], it's possible, for example, that slavery might have become an even more entrenched evil. And, although our air would have been cleaner and our climate less threatened, our forests and wilderness areas might have been more widely depleted. The pressure on the land would have been far greater because it would have been drawn upon for fuel as well as for food.

Coal is, as of this writing, at the center of the debate about the energy future of the world. China is one of the fastest growing economies in the world at the beginning of the twenty-first century. Its economic growth has largely been fueled by coal, as have its pollution and environmental problems. Environmental experts and organizations, including the United Nations Intergovernmental Panel on Climate Change (IPCC), worry that if China's model for economic development were followed by other developing nations, global warming would be impossible to halt. Coal resources, though, remain cheap and abundant in parts of Asia, the United States, and Latin America.

Newly industrialized nations of the nineteenth century chose to stabilize their economies and production around coal. That choice implies disregarding other choices.

[First president of the French republic] Napoléon III's Universal Exposition of 1867 in Paris showcased many of the newly engineered mechanical apparatuses of the age. One stood out. It was a large metallic conical construction, with an extended central post arising out of the cone's center, like the stamen at the center of a blooming flower. It looked like a giant ray gun, out of a science fiction story or like an oversized lampshade or umbrella pointed at the sky.

Augustin Mouchot was an obscure, nineteenth-century French mathematics academic from the countryside near the French city of Tours. He was the architect of the Exposition's "sun engine," as Parisian journalists dubbed it. The cone shape, made of copper sheets coated with burnished silver, captured sunlight and transferred it to a small boiler. Mouchot's solar reflector produced steam to drive a one-half horsepower engine to eighty strokes a minute. The boiler could also be used to operate a distilling unit that could vaporize five gallons of wine per minute. The only restrictions on the machine's energy use was the availability of sunlight and the amount it could harness based on its size.

The Exposition's visitors were fascinated with Mouchot's device because it required no fuel except the sun. It was a perpetual-motion machine, an engineering feat that no coal-fueled or steam-driven engine of the time could claim. Mouchot traveled to the French colony of Algiers to build solar collectors and to develop a method to produce energy from them when the sun did not shine. Although Mouchot enhanced his invention, he was never able to refine the apparatus's ability to function during long stretches of cloud cover. Coal mining increased throughout the French empire, due in part to more advanced mining techniques, and the ability of steam engine rail cars to transport coal long distances. These technologies, in turn, drove down fuel prices and spurred the economy.

The French government released a report in 1881, assessing solar energy's potential based on its sponsorship of two solar motors, one built by Mouchot and the other by one of his students, Abel Pifre. The report decided that solar energy was not practical for France because the sun was not equally available in all seasons, the cost was impractical compared to coal, and transport was difficult due to the complexity of large and fragile devices.

Mouchot's ideas continued to be published and discussed over the next 150 years. Some energy experts say we are, as of 2007, on the verge of a solar energy revolution. As with any revolution—solar, hydrogen, or clean coal technology—its success will be based on economics, environmental concerns, and humanity's desire to shape its future around a source of energy. The history of coal has already shown us that. Can coal again be the future of energy for the modern world? Whether one answers yes or no, another question quickly follows: Is coal use justified environmentally and economically? The viewpoints in the following chapters ask these fundamental questions about coal use, as well as whether coal use should be banned and whether coal mining is safe enough to justify its continuance.

OPPOSING
VIEWPOINTS®
SERIES

Is Coal the Future of Energy?

Chapter Preface

As of September 2003, 116 nations had signed the Kyoto protocol to reduce worldwide carbon emissions contributing to climate change, often called global warming. The Protocol, which went into effect in February 2005, was written to include a flexible system called carbon finance, or the "cap-and-trade" method. Many scientists believe that dense carbon emissions from one country can travel via the jet stream to another, causing adverse pollution and weather problems. A policy that rewards carbon emission reduction in one country would supposedly help all countries.

Carbon financing is simple economics applied to fossil fuel production and emission. There are two main components to the system:

1. Developed industrial nations, and those transitioning toward developed status, that are signatories to the Kyoto protocol, have agreed to limit their greenhouse gas emissions to an average of 5 percent below their 1990 levels by the year 2012, the measurement level at which emissions are "capped." These nations can make direct reductions in their fossil fuel emissions through regulation and innovation, or they can purchase surplus reductions from another developed nation that has reduced its emissions below their cap maximum. The surplus reduction credits are traded on an open market exchange called the Clean Development Mechanism (CDM). Developed nations use this economic activity to gradually lower *total* global fossil fuel emissions without legal sanctions and punishments.

2. Nondeveloped nations considering projects to generate economic and infrastructure growth, such as building electrical generating plants, are meant to benefit from

the CDM system. They are not subject to the Protocol's cap on emissions. But, crucially, they can sell emissions reductions to a developed country by substituting high-carbon emission projects with "green," low emission facilities and technologies prior to construction. CDM requires that the country prove that the construction of the electric energy facility, for example, would not have been possible without the purchase of certified emission credits from a developed nation. For instance, if the developing nation were considering building a coal-fired electrical generating plant, it might, instead, switch to a wind or hydropower generation. The country would then receive credits for the difference between the dense carbon emitting coal-based technology and small carbon output green project. The developing nation receives crucial money needed to build the project, provided by trading its energy emission credit under the cap and trade system.

The World Bank, through its Carbon Finance Unit (CFU), purchases emissions credits from developing countries, exchanging them for currency from developed nations who are over their emissions cap. The money then is transferred to the developing nation, contributing to their low-carbon construction project without requiring loans.

The CFU tracks potential emissions from energy projects around the globe. When it sees a developing project that has emission reduction potential, it brings to bear resources from 13 governments and 73 global private companies. For instance, if an economically challenged nation seeks to build an energy grid based on coal, the CFU will assess whether the same volume of energy could be produced using, for example, wind farms instead. Though it might be feasible, the country might argue that building wind farms would cost more to build than coal energy, and it does not have the technological infrastructure to build wind farms. The CFU acts as an intermediary, matching buyers (other developed countries seeking to purchase emissions reduction credits because they have gone over their emissions cap) to suppliers, the developing country. Negotiations begin: how many tons of carbon emissions will be reduced, how much the buyer will pay for the credits, the verification process, and so forth.

Some experts have argued that trading emissions credits merely benefits coal-based energy producers in developed countries because coal is a primary fuel for rapidly growing economies, in terms of price and availability, as of this writing. China, one of the world's fastest growing economies in 2007, is heavily invested in coal-based energy production. In the following chapter, various authors provide their viewpoints on whether coal merely delays the energy future or is, indeed, the world's best future source.

> *"New power plants are incorporating revolutionary new emission control equipment that could lead to a day when energy from coal can be produced pollution-free."*

Coal Will Be the Energy of the Future

U.S. Department of Energy, National Energy Technology Laboratory

In this viewpoint, researchers from the National Energy Technology Laboratory argue that there are technological advances that make it possible to reduce pollutants released when coal is burned. This viewpoint addresses five main pollutants of concern that need to be reduced in order for this to occur: soot, sulfur, nitrogen oxide, mercury, and carbon dioxide. While challenging, these obstacles can be overcome with technological innovations such as electrostatic precipitators and scrubbers that allow coal to burn in power plants with less pollution, making coal a promising energy of the future. The National Energy Technology Laboratory (NETL) is owned and operated by the U.S. Depart-

U.S. Department of Energy, "Secure & Reliable Energy Supplies—Coal Becomes a 'Future Fuel,'" *National Energy Technology Laboratory*. www.netl.doe.gov/KeyIssues/future_fuel.html, accessed August 8, 2007.

ment of Energy (DOE), and supports the DOE's mission to advance the national, economic, and energy security of the United States.

As you read, consider the following questions:

1. What is one of the new ways in which scientists and engineers have produced electricity from coal?
2. What are "scrubbers" and by how much can they reduce sulfur emissions?
3. What is the latest and most challenging of coal's environmental concerns?

Rising high above a reclaimed phosphate strip mine in southern Florida is a preview of coal's future. Within the gleaming steel towers of Tampa Electric Co.'s Polk Power Station, near Lakeland, Florida, are the latest—and to date, one of the most technologically advanced—of a series of innovations that make the plant one of the cleanest and most efficient coal plants operating anywhere in the world.

Many of these innovations can trace their engineering roots back a quarter century or more. In fact, for much of coal's modern history, technological progress has been defined by efforts to reduce pollutants released when coal is burned.

Most efforts to date have focused on cleaning pollutants from a coal boiler's "flue gas," the smoke produced by coal combustion. In recent years, however, scientists and engineers have developed entirely new ways to produce electricity from coal—for example, by first converting it to gas. This "new breed" of coal-fueled power plant offers plant owners unprecedented levels of operating efficiency—a benefit that, in turn, could help keep the costs of electricity to consumers affordable. Equally important, these new power plants are incorporating revolutionary new emission control equipment that could lead to a day when energy from coal can be produced pollution-free.

Eliminating Soot

In the early part of the 20th century, the primary concern was soot—the tiny particles of fly ash and dust that are expelled from coal-burning power plants. In 1923, the first electrostatic precipitator was used. It used electrical fields to remove particulate matter from a boiler's flue gas, much in the way that static electricity causes dust to cling to certain types of materials. Electrostatic precipitators, along with baghouses (which work like large industrial-scale vacuum cleaners to capture ash and dust particles in felt or woven fabric bags), have been able to reduce the release of soot-forming particulate matter by 99 percent or more. Today, all coal burning power plants employ one, or in some cases, both of these devices.

Scrubbing Out Sulfur

In the 1970s, sulfur and nitrogen oxides became the pollutants of most concern. Both combine with water vapor in the air to form dilute acids that can fall to earth as "acid rain."

Initially, some coal companies and power plant operators removed sulfur (as well as some of the ash-forming impurities in coal) from coal primarily by pre-cleaning it before it was burned; however, such "coal preparation" techniques were generally effective in reducing the sulfur content of coal by about only 25 percent. The sulfur that was present in coal in distinct particles (often bound with iron in the form of pyrite) could be removed by washing the coal, but such techniques had little effect on sulfur that was chemically bound to coal's carbon molecules.

The Clean Air Act of 1970 imposed more stringent pollution control requirements on coal-fired power plants. Although many coal-fired power plants attempted to comply with the new standards by building taller smokestacks to disperse the flue gases over a wider area or by burning lower sulfur coal, the legislation also accelerated research on a new type of pollution control device called a "flue gas desulfurization unit" or "scrubber." Rather than removing sulfur from coal before it was burned, scrubbers worked at the "back end" of a power plant, removing sulfur in the form of sulfur dioxide (or SO_2) that was present in the flue gas exiting the coal boiler.

Scrubbers can reduce sulfur emissions by 90 percent or more. They are essentially large towers in which aqueous mixtures of lime or limestone "sorbents" are sprayed through the flue gases exiting a coal boiler. The lime/limestone absorbs the sulfur from the flue gas.

Although some scrubbers had been built in Great Britain in the 1930s, it wasn't until 1967 that the first full-scale scrubber began operating in the United States at a coal-burning power plant. Early scrubbers experienced operating difficulties and cost overruns, but as the technology matured, their reliability and economics improved. Also, the first scrubbers converted the sulfur into a sludge-like waste product that could be difficult to handle; more recently, new treatment processes have been developed that produce a dry powder that can be used to make wallboard and for other commercial purposes.

In 1977 Congress passed a new Clean Air Act that essentially mandated that all new coal-fired power plants install scrubbers. By 1981, 52 of the Nation's 380 coal-burning utility plants had installed 84 scrubber systems. Today, more than 190 scrubbers are operating at 110 U.S. coal-fired power plants. Modern scrubbers have also shown varying degrees of effectiveness in reducing other pollutants, including particulates, acid gases, and in some cases, mercury and other heavy metals.

Knocking Out NOx

Nitrogen oxides also posed perplexing environmental challenges. Nitrogen oxides—or NOx—not only contribute to acid rain, they can also form harmful levels of ozone and reduce visibility. When coal burns, NOx forms from two sources: some nitrogen impurities embedded in coal's chemical structure combine with oxygen from the air to form NOx. In addition, the heat of combustion also causes nitrogen molecules in the air to break apart and undergo the same pollutant-forming reaction. In the late 1970s and 1980s, power plant engineers tested a new type of coal burner that fired coal in stages and carefully restricted the amount of oxygen in the stages where combustion temperatures were the highest. This concept of "staged combustion" led to "low-NOx burners." Low-NOx burners have been installed on nearly 75 percent of large U.S. coal-fired power plants. They have typically been effective in reducing nitrogen oxides by 40 to 60 percent.

In 1990, new amendments to the Clean Air Act mandated that nationwide caps be placed on the release of sulfur dioxide and nitrogen oxides from coal-burning power plants. In some areas of the United States—particularly the eastern portion of the Nation—many states must implement plans to reduce nitrogen oxides to even greater levels than those mandated by the nationwide cap. To reduce NOx pollutants to these levels, scientists have developed devices that work similar to a catalytic converter used to reduce automobile emissions. Called "selective catalytic reduction" systems, they are installed downstream of the coal boiler. Exhaust gases, prior to going up the smokestack, pass through the system where anhydrous ammonia reacts with the NOx and converts it to harmless nitrogen and water.

Some power plants are also injecting ammonia (or urea) directly into the coal furnace to reduce NOx. This technique, called "selective non-catalytic reduction," is much less expensive but also less effective than selective catalytic reduction.

Tackling Mercury

Today, mercury has joined the list of air pollutants of concern. Mercury is found in coal only in minute quantities, but when released during combustion, it can find its way into nearby water systems and accumulate in fish, creating a potential hu-

The Challenge of Global Carbon Capture

- Today fossil sources account for 80% of energy demand: Coal (25%), natural gas (21%), petroleum (34%), nuclear (6.5%), hydro (2.2%), and biomass and waste (11%). Only 0.4% of global energy demand is met by geothermal, solar and wind.

- 50% of the electricity generated in the U.S. is from coal.

- China is currently constructing the equivalent of two, 500 megawatt, coal-fired power plants per week and a capacity comparable to the entire UK power grid each year.

- One 500 megawatt coal-fired power plant produces approximately 3 million tons/year of carbon dioxide (CO_2).

- If all of this CO_2 is transported for sequestration, the quantity is equivalent to three times the weight and, under typical operating conditions, one-third of the annual volume of natural gas transported by the U.S. gas pipeline system.

- If 60% of the CO_2 produced from U.S. coal-based power generation were to be captured and compressed to a liquid for geologic sequestration, its volume would about equal the total U.S. oil consumption of 20 million barrels per day.

- At present the largest sequestration project is injecting one million tons/year of carbon dioxide (CO_2) from the Sleipner gas field into a saline aquifer under the North Sea.

John Deutch and Ernest J. Moniz, et al.,
"The Future of Coal: Options for a Carbon-constrained World,"
MIT Study on the Future of Coal,
Massachusetts Institute of Technology, 2007, http://web.mit.edu/coal.

man health problem. The challenge is that mercury can be released from a coal plant in several different chemical forms, depending on the type of coal burned and the type of power plant equipment.

In some cases, flue gas desulfurization units, or baghouses and electrostatic precipitators can help reduce mercury emissions; but with certain coals and plant configurations, these devices may be completely ineffective. Scientists are working on new ways to modify existing pollution control devices or develop new ones that use special sorbents for reducing mercury emissions. For example, activated carbon—a substance commonly used to remove odors and contaminants in drinking water systems—has also been shown to be effective in absorbing mercury from the flue gases of coal plants. The mercury clings to the activated carbon particles and can be removed by downstream particulate control devices such as electrostatic precipitators. Research is also underway to study other chemicals that could be added to the coal or injected into the flue gas to enhance mercury capture.

A New Way to Burn Coal

For much of coal's modern history, technological innovations have focused on ways to reduce pollutants after they have been released from the coal boiler. But beginning in the mid-1960s, engineers began studying an entirely different approach to controlling emissions—reducing them inside the boiler itself. The concept came to be known as fluidized-bed combustion.

Rather than the traditional way of burning coal—blowing pulverized particles of coal into a super-hot (approx. 3,000 degrees F) combustion chamber—fluidized-bed combustors suspend larger chunks of coal (about the size of your fingernail) on upward-blowing jets of air. Suspended on this cushion of air, the "bed" of coal tumbles as it burns, taking on many of the characteristics of a boiling liquid, hence the name "fluidized bed."

The turbulent mixing process allows coal to be burned efficiently at lower temperatures, reducing the formation of nitrogen oxides. The lower temperatures (1,200–1,400 degrees F) also are ideal for mixing limestone (or a similar substance called dolomite) in with the coal to absorb sulfur dioxide and convert it into a dry powdery form that can be removed with the coal ash. Fluidized-bed combustors are effective in reducing sulfur and nitrogen oxide pollutants by more than 90 percent, they eliminate the need for a post-combustion scrubber, and they can burn almost any grade of coal.

The first fluidized bed combustors were used in smaller industrial plants and for local heating systems; today, the technology has been scaled up and is used in several multi-hundred-megawatt commercial power plants. More than 170 fluidized-bed combustion units now operate in the United States.

These technological advances helped coal-burning utilities sharply reduce air pollutants even as they have substantially increased their use of coal. From 1980 to 2003, the amount of coal used to generate electricity in the United States increased by 75 percent; however, during the same time period, sulfur dioxide and nitrogen oxide emissions declined by 40 percent. At the same time, existing pollution controls reduced mercury emissions by 40 percent below levels that would have been emitted had there been no pollution controls on power plants.

The Coal Plant of the Future

A new breed of coal plant that relies on coal gasification represents an important trend in coal-fired units—distinctly different from the conventional coal combustion power station. Rather than burning coal, such plants first convert coal into a combustible gas. The conversion process—achieved by reacting coal with steam and oxygen under high pressures—produces a gas that can be cleaned of more than 99 percent of its sulfur and nitrogen impurities using processes common to the modern chemical industry. Trace elements of mercury and other potential pollutants can also be removed from the coal gas; in fact, the coal gas can be cleaned to purity levels approaching, or in some cases, surpassing those of natural gas.

These new plants also achieve unprecedented efficiencies by generating two sources of electricity. Once cleaned, the coal gases are burned in a gas turbine-generator—again much like natural gas—to produce one source of electricity. Exhaust gases exiting the turbine are hot enough to boil water, creating steam that drives a conventional steam turbine-generator, producing a second source of electricity. This dual combination of gas and steam turbine systems accounts for the technology's name: integrated gasification combined-cycle.

Integrated gasification combined-cycle power plants are one of the cleanest and most efficient coal-fueled power stations. Not only will they be able to eliminate virtually all of coal's-pollutants, they will be able to generate considerably more power from a given quantity of coal. Today's power plants, for example, extract only about 33–35 percent of the energy value of coal. Because of their dual means for generating electric power, future integrated gasification combined-cycle plants may be capable of extracting up to 60 percent of coal's energy. Higher coal-to-electricity efficiencies mean that less coal is used to generate power; and when less coal is used, less carbon dioxide is emitted.

A Climate Change Solution

Carbon dioxide is the latest—and certainly the most challenging—of coal's environmental concerns. Boosting power plant efficiencies is currently the most cost-effective way to reduce carbon dioxide, but it will likely not be sufficient to substantially reduce the threat of global climate change. For large-scale carbon dioxide reductions, it will likely be necessary to capture these emissions from the exhausts of coal plants and safely prevent them from entering the atmosphere.

Within the last decade, many of the world's coal and power plant researchers have begun studying ways to capture and dispose of carbon dioxide. Their efforts have led to a new family of promising carbon sequestration technologies. With carbon sequestration, it may be possible to safely and permanently store carbon dioxide from coal plants directly in deep geologic formations, perhaps in unmineable coal seams or in depleted oil or gas fields, or indirectly in forests and soils. Longer-range research is also showing exciting possibilities for converting carbon dioxide into environmentally safe solid minerals that could be returned to the earth, perhaps to the same mines from which the coal was extracted.

A key to successful carbon sequestration will be to find affordable ways to separate carbon dioxide from the exhaust gases of coal plants. Techniques are being developed that can be applied to conventional combustion plants, but it is likely that capture methods will be even more effective when applied to integrated gasification combined-cycle plants. Integrated gasification combined-cycle plants release carbon dioxide in a much more concentrated stream than conventional plants, making its capture more effective and affordable.

Today, as a result of these technological advancements, the concept of a pollution-free, highly efficient coal-fueled power plant is no longer confined to an engineer's drawing board. The basic equipment for this new breed of coal plant is being developed and tested, much of it at large scales. No longer is the coal plant of the future just a utility company's dream; today such plants are taking shape, and because of the new technology they will employ, the future of coal—like our Nation's air—is becoming clearer.

| "Carbon dioxide emissions from coal burning have been increasing, up to 24 percent since 1990."

Coal Should Not Be the Energy of the Future

Travis Madsen and Rob Sargent

The authors of this viewpoint, Travis Madsen and Rob Sargent, argue that coal should not be the future of energy production. Coal's abundance does not justify its pollution potential to effect dangerous climate change. They argue that new, technologically advanced coal-firing plants are almost as polluting as old ones and add to detrimental health consequences from emissions. The financial risks inherent in coal production and use are little discussed by coal proponents, according to the authors. Travis Madsen is an energy policy analyst, and Rob Sargent is a senior policy analyst with U.S. Public Interest Research Group (PIRG).

As you read, consider the following questions:

1. Should the global average temperature rise 3.6 degrees Fahrenheit above preindustrial levels, what would be the consequences, according to the authors?

2. According to the authors, coal is responsible for what percentage of carbon dioxide emissions in the United States?

3. What is the major problem with coal gasification technology as a means to reduce carbon emissions, according to the viewpoint authors?

Construction of new coal-fired power plants on . . . a massive scale would extend U.S. overdependence on coal for another half-century, with major impacts on America's environment and economy. It would commit the U.S. to an enormous increase in global warming pollution; risk financial harm to individual power companies, ratepayers and the U.S. economy; damage wide areas of land and foul water supplies with mining waste; and create health-threatening air and water pollution. Furthermore, staking America's energy future on coal would consume billions of dollars that could otherwise promote more sustainable energy sources.

Increased Global Warming Pollution

A new fleet of coal-fired power plants will dramatically increase U.S. global warming pollution, increasing the severity of the impact of global warming on current and future generations of Americans.

Global warming threatens to significantly increase temperatures across America and around the world, causing dramatic changes in our economy and quality of life. Vast amounts of scientific evidence show that global warming is happening, and that human activity is the primary cause.

By burning fossil fuels, humans have changed the composition of the atmosphere. As a result, it now traps more of the sun's heat near the Earth's surface. The leading culprit is carbon dioxide, the product of fossil fuel combustion. Carbon dioxide levels in the atmosphere are now increasing faster than at any time in the last 20,000 years, and are likely higher now than at any point in the last 20 million years.

As carbon dioxide levels have risen, global temperatures have increased. In the last century, global average temperatures rose by about 1.4 degrees Fahrenheit [F]—an unprecedented event in the past thousand years. The 1990s were the warmest decade in a millennium and 2005 was the hottest year in over a century of recordkeeping.

The Disaster Above 3.6° F

This warming trend cannot be explained by natural variables—such as solar cycles or volcanic eruptions. However, it does correspond to models of climate change based on human influence.

The Intergovernmental Panel on Climate Change (IPCC) predicts that global average temperatures could rise by between 2.5° and 10.4° F by the end of the century, depending on how society responds to the threat. Recent research suggests that the IPCC may have underestimated the extent to which feedback loops could increase the warming effect— meaning that temperatures could actually rise by as much as 14° F by 2100.

Climate scientists warn that the world faces dire environmental consequences unless we find a way to quickly and rapidly reduce our emissions of global warming pollutants.

Many scientists and policy-makers (such as the European Union) recognize a 3.6° F (2° Celsius) increase in global average temperatures over pre-industrial levels as a rough limit beyond which large-scale, dangerous impacts of global warming would become unavoidable. Even below 3.6° F, significant impacts from global warming are likely, such as damage to many ecosystems, decreases in crop yields, sea level rise, and the widespread loss of coral reefs.

Beyond 3.6° F, however, the impacts of global warming become much more severe, including some or all of the following impacts:

- Eventual loss of the Greenland ice sheet, triggering a sea-level rise of 7 meters over the next millennium (and possibly much faster);

- A further increase in the intensity of hurricanes;

- Loss of 97 percent of the world's coral reefs;

- Displacement of tens of millions of people due to sea level rise;

- Total loss of Arctic summer sea ice;

- Expansion of insect-borne disease;

- Greater risk of positive feedback effects—such as the release of methane stored in permafrost—that could lead to even greater warming in the future.

Carbon Fuel Danger

At temperature increases of 5 to 7° F, far more dramatic shifts would take place, including:

- Increased potential for shutdown of the thermohaline circulation, which carries warmth from the tropics to Europe;

- Increased potential for melting of the West Antarctic ice sheet, triggering an eventual 5 to 6 meter rise in sea level;

- Major crop failures in many parts of the world;

- Extreme disruptions to ecosystems.

In addition, the more global temperatures rise, the greater the risks of abrupt climate change increase. The historical climate record includes many instances in which the world's climate shifted dramatically in the course of decades, even years—with local temperature changes of as much as 18° F in 10 years.

Should the world continue on its current course, with fossil fuel consumption continuing to rise, temperature would likely increase beyond the threshold for dangerous climate change—and continue to rise for generations to come.

Stabilizing CO_2 Levels

Minimizing the threat of global warming requires deep cuts in global warming pollution. To have a reasonable chance of keeping global temperatures from rising by more than 3.6° F, the atmospheric concentration of carbon dioxide must be held below 450 parts per million (ppm)—about 60 percent higher than pre-industrial levels and about 18 percent higher than today. Holding concentrations below 400 ppm would be even more effective.

To stabilize carbon dioxide levels at 450 ppm, however, the world will need to halt the growth of global warming pollution in this decade, begin reducing emissions soon, and slash emissions by more than half by 2050. Greater reductions would be required to limit carbon dioxide levels to 400 ppm. Because the U.S. is the world's largest global warming polluter, the degree of emission reductions required here will be greater. For example, the European Union has set a goal of cutting emissions by 15 to 30 percent below 1990 levels by 2020 and 60 to 80 percent by 2050. To the extent that current forecasts underestimate the potential for feedback loops to trigger greater warming, pollution may have to be cut deeper and more rapidly to stave off the worst effects.

If U.S. power companies build a new fleet of coal-fired power plants—even a fraction of the proposed number—it will become far more difficult to achieve reductions in global warming pollution on this scale.

The "Coal Rush" and Global Warming

Coal has an oversized impact on global warming. Burning coal in a conventional coal-fired power plant is the most carbon-intensive way to generate a kilowatt-hour of electricity.

In 1999, coal-fired power plants in the U.S. produced over 2 pounds of carbon dioxide per kWh [kilowatt-hour; one watt is the amount of electrical energy expended by a one-watt load (i.e., a light bulb) drawing power for one hour, kilowatt is 10^5 watt hours, and usually refers to residential electrical usage], while gas-fired plants produced over a third less. Coal is responsible for 84 percent of all carbon dioxide pollution from electricity generation in the U.S.

Overall, coal is responsible for about one-third of all emissions of carbon dioxide in America. Indeed, carbon dioxide emissions from coal-fired power generation in America alone exceed the total emissions of any nation in the world, except China. Further, carbon dioxide emissions from coal burning have been increasing, up 24 percent since 1990.

The "coal rush" would drastically increase U.S. global warming pollution. If all of the planned [as of 2006] coal-fired power plants are built, they would increase annual electricity-related carbon dioxide pollution by more than 25 percent above 2004 levels (an increase of 590 million metric tons). This translates to a 10 percent increase in overall U.S. carbon dioxide pollution (compared to 2004) and a 2.4 percent increase in global emissions. Assuming plants built during the coal rush have 60-year lifetimes, they would emit over 35 billion metric tons of global warming pollution.

New Coal-Fired Power Plants: Same as the Old Ones

Proponents of coal as an energy source often point to coal gasification technology as an environmentally responsible way to use coal, with lower overall pollution. For example, General Electric has been running a series of television advertisements promoting its "clean coal" technology as a way to solve America's energy problems.

Gasified coal technology, such as integrated gasification combined cycle (IGCC) [integrated gasification combined

Proposed Coal-Fired Power Plants by Type (as of 2006)		
Technology	Number	Percentage
Conventional Pulverized Coal	89	59%
Coal Gasification (IGCC)	25	16%
Circulating Fluidized Bed	22	15%
Supercritical Pulverized Coal	10	7%
To Be Determined	5	3%

TAKEN FROM: Madsen and Sargent, "Making Sense of the 'Coal Rush,'" U.S. PIRG, July 2006, www.pirg.org.

cycle technology turns coal into gas, called syngas, generating electricity. Steam produced from the syngas is recovered and produces additional electricity], does have some modest advantages over conventional pulverized coal technology: it is slightly more efficient and has lower emissions of conventional pollutants. In addition, gasification technology transforms coal into a mixture of gases before burning it, making it possible to capture carbon dioxide before it heads up the smokestack. The federal government, in partnership with the power industry, is studying the possibility of storing carbon dioxide in large quantities underground [called CO_2 capture and sequestration(ces)]—which would theoretically allow for the production of low- or zero-carbon power from coal.

But while IGCC technology may be the one option for the coal industry to demonstrate it can be part of a global warming solution, there is one problem: gasification plants are not the kind of coal plants electricity companies are proposing to build.

Only 16 percent of currently proposed coal-fired power plants would use gasification technology, and only the Department of Energy's FutureGen demonstration plant is proposed to incorporate carbon capture and storage. Most of the proposed plants use conventional design. As a result, many of the coal plants, if built, will not be well suited to the carbon capture and storage process that many see as the only way to use coal without a huge increase in global warming pollution.

Even if all of the new coal-fired power plants were to use gasification technology with carbon storage, the approach remains expensive, and no industry or country has yet demonstrated the feasibility of permanently storing billions of tons of carbon dioxide underground.

In sum, the "coal rush" now being planned by electricity companies does not match up with the rhetoric touting coal as a clean and environmentally friendly source of power. Rather, it would commit the U.S. to the expansion of traditional coal-fired power plant technology and to a large increase in global warming pollution. At a time when policymakers and scientists across the world are struggling to find ways to avoid the most dangerous effects of global warming, allowing the coal rush to take place as planned would be beyond unwise—it would be thoroughly reckless and irresponsible.

Gasified Coal and Global Warming

Some energy companies are promoting gasified coal as an environmentally responsible way to use coal to generate electricity. However, high costs and technological hurdles make this technology less than ideal as a solution to global warming.

Coal gasification is more expensive than cleaner and more sustainable ways of addressing our nation's energy-related and environmental problems. Coal gasification with carbon storage is more than twice as expensive as typical energy efficiency measures and more than 50 percent more costly than the best wind power projects. Even without carbon storage, the most optimistic forecasts by the research arm of the electric industry, the Electric Power Research Institute (EPRI), put the price of coal gasification at around 4.7 cents per kWh in 2010—close to 200 percent more expensive than a well-executed energy efficiency program. However, EPRI predicts that the average cost of wind power will drop 30 percent between 2010 and 2020, and by 2020, both wind and biomass energy will be significantly cheaper than any type of coal power plant with carbon storage.

Moreover, carbon capture and storage—on the scale at which it must be implemented to fight global warming—is an immature technology with serious questions about its future viability. Carbon dioxide has been injected into the ground for some time to enhance oil recovery. However, the storage of captured carbon dioxide from utility operations would require a vast expansion of carbon transportation infrastructure and identification of storage locations with huge capacity. Storing all U.S. power plant coal emissions would require enough infrastructure to liquefy, transport and inject roughly 2 billion metric tons of carbon dioxide annually. Currently, there are only 21 demonstration projects in the world, and not one of them is large enough to store the lifetime emissions of even one power plant.

Storing any quantity of carbon dioxide presents problems. As with nuclear wastes, carbon dioxide stored in geological formations must be guaranteed to remain underground for hundreds or thousands of years to prevent re-release to the atmosphere and to prevent accidental, large-scale releases of carbon dioxide, which can be fatal to humans and wildlife. Recent studies indicate that carbon dioxide acidifies saline aquifers, which can degrade some of the concrete-like minerals that seal holes in the rock, or concrete plugs in old oil and gas wells, raising questions about the permanence of storage. Ocean storage, which has been considered a possible option for carbon management, appears less attractive given recent research tying increasing ocean carbon dioxide levels with acidification and damage to ocean ecosystems.

Provided that the technological hurdles can be overcome, IGCC will likely only become a key player in the energy mix if policies are in place to make it economically competitive with conventional coal technology. A carbon cap that places a market price on carbon dioxide emissions from power plants could provide an incentive for cleaner technologies such as IGCC to develop. Even then, however, IGCC power plants would only deliver global warming benefits by replacing existing dirty and inefficient coal-fired power plants—not by adding to them.

Economic Coal Risk and Pollution

Increasing America's dependence on coal carries significant economic risk for electricity companies, municipally and co-operatively owned utilities, ratepayers and shareholders, and for the economy as a whole.

Any new coal-fired power plants would be built in the face of incontrovertible evidence that carbon dioxide emissions are causing the planet to warm. There is growing consensus, even within the United States, that concerted action must soon be taken to curb global warming emissions. . . .

Financial Risk

As global warming pollution limits are set, coal-fired power plants will decline in value compared to less-polluting resources. Additionally, companies or ratepayers may be forced to pay the significant cost of retrofitting the new plants to capture and store carbon dioxide.

Some electricity resource planners argue that future costs associated with global warming regulations are too uncertain, and thus leave estimates out of planning decisions altogether. However, this omission effectively assigns future carbon emissions a cost of zero—which is not accurate, especially not over the 50 years a new power plant could operate. According to a recent analysis by Synapse Energy Economics, one ton of carbon dioxide pollution will likely cost between $10 and $40 in 2010; and between $20 and $50 in 2030. Synapse bases its calculations on relatively modest policy proposals that have been made to date—not on the more stringent emission cuts that will be necessary to avoid the most dangerous consequences of global warming.

Companies that choose to move forward with coal-fired plants in the face of this knowledge expose themselves, their shareholders and their ratepayers to a substantial economic risk. Owners of coal-fired power plants could be required to pay for the right to emit carbon dioxide into the environment—either through a carbon tax designed to reduce emissions or through the purchase of pollution permits in an emission trading scheme. In either case, the cost of producing electricity from coal-fired power plants would increase and the value of those plants relative to other, less carbon-intensive forms of generation would decline.

Another possible scenario is that coal-fired power plant owners would be required to install equipment to capture and store carbon dioxide emissions from the plant. Such investments are likely to be very expensive. The Electric Power Research Institute (EPRI) estimates that energy from a conventional coal-fired power plant would cost 77 percent more with carbon capture and storage. Pulverized coal plants would become much more expensive than gasified coal after rules requiring carbon capture and storage are implemented. (Because carbon sequestration is untested on a large scale, it could prove even more expensive than estimated by EPRI.)

Passing on the Coal Cost

Depending on the regulatory scheme governing the particular company involved, these additional costs would be passed down [to consumers]. Allocation of these costs could provoke significant battles. In the 1980s, state PUCs [Public Utility Commissions] and consumer advocates fought heated battles with utilities over the allocation of costs for the construction of nuclear power plants, in some cases arguing that the decision to invest in nuclear power was "imprudent," and that the utilities should not be permitted to recover excess costs from ratepayers.

Shareholders are unlikely to want to pay the additional costs either, and are beginning to demand that corporate directors consider their exposure to global warming-related risks. Shareholders of major companies filed 30 resolutions in 2005 requesting planning or action to reduce the risk of global warming. And insurance companies have been considering reforms to reflect the risk, including denying liability coverage for directors and officers of companies sued for mismanagement over global warming.

Municipal and cooperatively owned utilities face the same risk by choosing coal-fired power. In the event of a reduction in the value of their assets or an increase in costs caused by future climate regulation, these utilities would have to pass on costs to their members and ratepayers.

In addition, credit rating agencies may lower the bond ratings of companies that ignore the risk associated with future carbon regulation. With a lower bond rating, a company must pay higher interest rates in order to obtain a loan and would likely pass the increased cost of capital onto its customers.

While the scope and stringency of future global warming regulations have yet to be decided, companies investing in coal-fired power plants know that carbon dioxide regulation is right around the corner. Investing in coal-fired power plants under the assumption that carbon dioxide will remain unregulated is imprudent, and is a recipe for future exposure to financial and regulatory risk. . . .

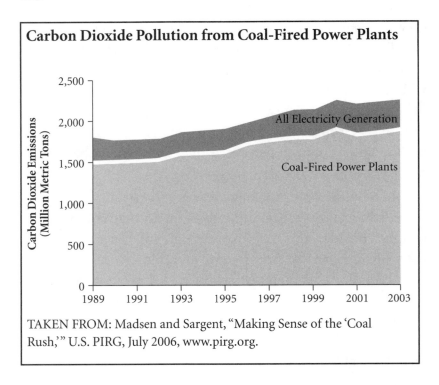

Carbon Dioxide Pollution from Coal-Fired Power Plants

TAKEN FROM: Madsen and Sargent, "Making Sense of the 'Coal Rush,'" U.S. PIRG, July 2006, www.pirg.org.

More Health-Threatening Pollution

If all of the planned coal-fired power plants are built, they would increase annual pollution from power plants and other industrial facilities on the order of 1 to 3 percent. These plants would directly emit an estimated:

- 120,000 tons per year of sulfur dioxide, a major ingredient in fine particle pollution, linked to premature death and respiratory and cardiovascular disease;

- 240,000 tons per year of nitrogen dioxide, a major ingredient in the photochemical smog that plagues many cities across the U.S. on summer days, triggering asthma attacks and sending people to the hospital; and

- 3 tons per year of mercury, a neurological toxicant that contaminates fish in rivers, lakes and the oceans.

Because new coal-fired power plants will have to meet modern air pollution standards under the federal Clean Air Act, air pollution from new coal-fired power plants will be improved compared to the oldest coal-fired plants. However, coal-fired power is still far from clean—especially compared to non-polluting energy sources including energy efficiency and wind power.

Adding to the pollution problem, increased coal freight shipments will create more diesel soot across the country.

Lost Opportunities for Clean Energy

The "coal rush" would consume investment dollars that could be used to promote cheaper and cleaner energy sources, including energy efficiency and renewable power.

In order to build all of the coal-fired power plants on the drawing board [as of 2006], electric utilities would have to invest $137 billion in capital costs. On top of this investment, utilities would have to spend over $100 billion to operate and maintain the plants, purchase fuel and build transmission lines to carry the power. Future regulation of global warming pollution would create additional expenditures. In addition, the "coal rush" would also tend to drive billions of dollars in capital investment from other actors—for example, mining companies and railroads. Ultimately, this money will come out of the pockets of public taxpayers, ratepayers and investors.

However, by investing in coal, America would lose a golden opportunity. If that same $137 billion in capital were instead invested in a balanced clean energy strategy, including energy efficient and renewable technologies like wind power, it could produce a similar amount of energy (or more), while creating practically zero global warming pollution, safeguarding the economy from risks associated with global warming, reducing mining impacts and greatly cutting health-threatening air pollution. In addition, investment in renewables and efficiency would generate jobs, renew communities, and help to stabilize energy prices.

| "Clean coal technologies will play a vital role in the future well-being of the U.S."

Coal Is the Best Energy Security Option

Carl O. Bauer

Carl O. Bauer argues in this viewpoint that coal will continue to be the dominant fossil fuel for the foreseeable future. He argues for government research and development as a means to rapidly advance creative coal technologies to help mitigate the cost and pollution potential of coal-burning plants. The future is not only coal, but also, Bauer argues, the ability to use coal in a multi-faceted and technologically advanced way that will secure fuel supplies and U.S. energy security. Carl O. Bauer is the director of the National Energy Technology Laboratory at the U.S. Department of Energy in Pittsburgh, Pennsylvania.

As you read, consider the following question:

1. The U.S. Department of Energy (DOE) and the National Energy Technology Laboratory support what kind of research and development for the coal industry, according to the viewpoint?

2. According to the author, the Eastman Chemical Company has been using clean gasification production for over twenty years. The author believes the coal industry must duplicate Eastman's success because it would reduce what major pollutant?

3. Should DOE's FutureGen project succeed, it will produce the world's first coal-powered energy plant of its kind. What will its environmental benefit be, according to the viewpoint?

Our nation is heavily dependent on fossil fuels for electricity production, with coal, natural gas and petroleum accounting for more than 70 percent of today's total, and coal alone accounting for nearly 50 percent [as of 2006].

The Energy Information Administration (EIA) projects that coal will remain the dominant fuel for the foreseeable future. Domestically coal is the most abundant, reliable and economical of the three fossil fuels. To meet growing energy demand, maintain competitive and secure energy, and sustain economic growth, the United States must continue to rely on its proven coal reserves. In addition, coal can serve as the bridge to the hydrogen economy. However, for coal to remain a source of clean, affordable and secure energy, advances in energy conversion systems are necessary.

A Major Success in Coal Technology

The U.S. Department of Energy (DOE), through the National Energy Technology Laboratory (NETL), supports R&D [research and development] in advanced, cost-effective combustion, gasification and environmental control technologies for the existing fleet of coal-based power plants, as well as new generation systems. Further, the R&D program provides a roadmap to energy production in the future, with associated projects that will lead to near zero-emissions coal-based en-

The Economic Benefits for Coal-Based Energy

On March 22nd, [2006,] the National Coal Council (NCC) released a study entitled "Coal: America's Energy Future," containing recommendations to the U.S. Secretary of Energy. . . .

The study recommends the additional use of coal to reduce U.S. energy costs 33%, while creating more than 1 million new American jobs per year and achieving an aggregate gain of more than $3 trillion in gross domestic product (GDP). It also identifies ample amounts of U.S. coal reserves to support 100 gigawatts of new electricity generation, 2.6 million barrels per day of refined liquid products and 4 trillion cubic feet per year of natural gas production, in addition to supporting ethanol, enhanced recovery of oil and coalbed methane and hydrogen production.

American Coal Council. "National Coal Council Study—'Coal: America's Energy Future," *Newsletter, November 2006. www.clean-coal.info.*

ergy plants. These activities directly support the President's [George W. Bush] National Energy Policy and the 2005 Energy Bill.

The improvement in coal-based power generation embodied by gasification-based systems is a major success in technology development, spurred by increasingly stringent pollution control standards, the need to reduce carbon dioxide (CO_2) emissions and the flexibility to utilize a wide variety of feedstocks while co-producing electricity, fuels and chemicals. Coal-based gasification systems have been proven capable of achieving extremely low levels of pollutant discharges to the environment, setting a new standard for coal-based power plants. Moreover, its inherently higher efficiency significantly reduces the discharge of all pollutants, including greenhouse gases, per megawatt-hour [equal to 10^6 watts, used for metering large amounts of electrical energy, i.e., a power plant] of electricity generated.

Gasification technologies were developed in the late 18th century. In the 19th century, gasification was used extensively for the production of "town gas" for urban areas. Although the availability of pipeline natural gas has made this application obsolete, gasification has found new applications in the production of fuels and chemicals and in large-scale power production. For example, gasification has been a part of Eastman Chemical Company's chemical complex in Kingsport, Tenn., for over 20 years. They have demonstrated the ability to produce a clean syngas that is used as a chemical "building block" for a wide range of consumer products. Of particular significance, Eastman has been removing [more than] 95 percent of the mercury from its syngas, using relatively inexpensive sulfur-impregnated activated carbon technology for nearly 20 years, while mercury control from conventional pulverized coal (PC) [burning coal, that has been finely crushed, in a standard boiler] power plants is still in its infancy.

DOE has been instrumental in the development of coal-based gasification systems for power generation, known as integrated gasification combined cycle (IGCC) [technological process of converting coal to gas and using the gas, and its steam emissions, to generate electricity more efficiently than PC plants]. The first two coal-based IGCC plants built in the U.S.—Wabash River and Polk Power Station—were demonstrated through the Clean Coal Technology Demonstration Program in the late '90s and early 2000s. DOE continues to contribute to IGCC development with the selection of the Excelsior Energy and Southern Company Services projects in Round 2 of the Clean Coal Power Initiative (CCPI).

Improvements to PC plants also are part of the DOE R&D portfolio. Although early subcritical PC plants had efficiencies of around 20 percent, the average operating efficiency for today's plants is around 33–35 percent. Starting in the 1960s, super-critical PC plants (operating at 3,600 psig [pounds per square inch gauge] and 1,100° F) were developed and deployed in the U.S., and these units had efficiencies approaching 40 percent. Construction materials are the main impediment to reaching even higher steam temperatures. Ongoing research is aimed at developing advanced materials that will allow steam cycles to be extended even further, to the ultra-supercritical range, with pressures and temperatures approaching 5,000 psig and 1,400° F, respectively. The higher steam temperatures will equate to increased cycle efficiency, and ultimately, fewer emissions.

Oxy-combustion is another developing technology that holds promise for reducing NOx [nitrogen oxide] emissions and enabling carbon capture. In oxy-combustion, oxygen rather than air is used to combust a fuel resulting in a highly pure CO_2 exhaust that can be captured at relatively low cost. The major obstacle to oxy-combustion is the cost of generating a large volume of nearly pure oxygen. DOE is funding research that is investigating low-cost methods for producing pure oxygen. This is an example of a cross-cutting R&D activity since a nearly pure oxygen stream is also a prerequisite for most gasification technologies.

FutureGen and Coal

A major DOE initiative is the FutureGen program, which will be the culmination of many intensive research efforts and will result in the world's first near-zero emission coal-based power plant. FutureGen is a 275-MW [megawatt], gasification-based plant that will produce hydrogen and electricity in a combined cycle mode. The $1 billion DOE industry partnership will provide the technical and economic basis for co-producing electricity and hydrogen from the nation's abundant supply of coal, while at the same time capturing and sequestering CO_2.

FutureGen is scheduled to begin operating in 2012 and virtually every aspect of the prototype plant will be based on cutting-edge technology. Technologies planned for testing at the plant, if successful, could provide future electric power generation with near-zero emissions at a cost only 10 percent higher than today's electricity. FutureGen will also generate a highly enriched hydrogen gas that can be burned more cleanly than coal. Alternatively, hydrogen can be used in a fuel cell to produce ultra-clean electricity, fed to a refinery to help upgrade petroleum products or used to demonstrate its effectiveness as a transportation fuel.

Energy security and energy independence are [George W. Bush's] presidential priorities. Environmental performance is a much greater factor now than in the past as emission standards tighten and market growth occurs in areas where total allowable emissions are capped. The reduction of CO_2 emissions is one of the major challenges facing industry in response to concerns over global climate change. To help meet these challenges, there is a need for more environmentally sound, flexible, efficient and reliable systems that remain cost effective in competitive markets. Advanced coal-based technologies are poised to meet these requirements.

A MultiPurpose Coal Future

The majority of existing applications are geared toward the production of a single product (electricity). The potential of tomorrow's advanced coal-based technologies is promising because of their ability to use low-cost and blended feedstocks, their ability to produce multiple products and their exemplary environmental profile. With escalating natural gas prices and increased security and environmental concerns, advanced coal-based power generation technologies will become the cornerstone for market flexibility. As they do, advanced technologies will also reduce capital, operating and maintenance costs of coal-based plants, achieve near-zero emissions of all pollutants, demonstrate higher thermal efficiencies and capture CO_2.

Further deployment of these advanced technologies will allow coal to continue to support our energy infrastructure while helping to sustain a clean environment. Clean coal technologies will play a vital role in the future well-being of the U.S. The same dynamics that make clean coal technologies attractive in the U.S. will apply in many other regions of the world. As a result of DOE's R&D programs, the U.S. is in a position to serve a significant segment of the global market for clean coal technologies. Exporting these technologies will help the U.S. improve its balance of trade and increase employment opportunities. It will also help other nations to achieve a common goal: a cleaner environment.

> *"If the ration of coal to nuclear were re-*
> *versed so that only 20 percent of our*
> *electricity were generated from coal and*
> *60 percent from nuclear, this would go*
> *a long way toward cleaning the air."*

Coal Is the Wrong Energy Security Option

Patrick Moore

Patrick Moore, cofounder of the environmental group Green-
peace, is chairman and chief scientist of Greenspirit Strategies
Ltd. In this viewpoint, Moore discusses how he has reversed his
former opposition to nuclear power. He believes in using nuclear
power in opposition to a coal-based future. Coupled with alter-
native energies, nuclear power can safely meet the growing de-
mand for energy while reducing the detrimental, carbon-based
pollution of coal-fired generators, Moore argues. While we can-
not shield ourselves from the dangers of nuclear power, he writes,
they are less dangerous than perceived, and much less dangerous
to the planet than coal-based energy platforms.

As you read, consider the following questions:

1. Why does author Patrick Moore believe nuclear power should replace coal-based power plants?
2. Who are the other environmentalists Moore cites as having changed their minds about nuclear power?
3. How do deaths from coal mining compare to deaths from nuclear accidents, according to the viewpoint?

In the early 1970s when I helped found Greenpeace [an international environmental organization], I believed that nuclear energy was synonymous with nuclear holocaust, as did most of my compatriots. That's the conviction that inspired Greenpeace's first voyage up the spectacular rocky northwest coast to protest the testing of U.S. hydrogen bombs in Alaska's Aleutian Islands. Thirty years on, my views have changed, and the rest of the environmental movement needs to update its views, too, because nuclear energy may just be the energy source that can save our planet from another possible disaster: catastrophic climate change.

Look at it this way: More than 600 coal-fired electric plants in the United States produce 36 percent of U.S. emissions—or nearly 10 percent of global emissions—of CO_2 [carbon dioxide], the primary greenhouse gas responsible for climate change. Nuclear energy is the only large-scale, cost-effective energy source that can reduce these emissions while continuing to satisfy a growing demand for power. And these days it can do so safely.

I say that guardedly, of course, just days after Iranian President Mahmoud Ahmadinejad [in 2006] announced that his country had enriched uranium. "The nuclear technology is only for the purpose of peace and nothing else," he said. But there is widespread speculation that, even though the process is ostensibly dedicated to producing electricity, it is in fact a cover for building nuclear weapons.

Reduce Coal Consumption

The obvious place for the U.S. to start reducing its greenhouse gases is with the coal that produces half our electricity. We now burn coal twice as much as we did when [President] Jimmy Carter set out to solve our energy problems in the late 1970s. (In fact, Mr. Carter promoted coal.) Our coal consumption now produces 10% of the world's carbon dioxide. Replacing a good portion of our coal plants over the next 25 years would be the surest way of addressing the problem.

William Tucker, "How to Make the Rhetoric Less Heated, and the Planet Too," Wall Street Journal, June 8, 2006, www.wsj.com.

And although I don't want to underestimate the very real dangers of nuclear technology in the hands of rogue states, we cannot simply ban every technology that is dangerous. That was the all-or-nothing mentality at the height of the Cold War [period of conflict, tension, and competition between the United States and Soviet Union from 1947–1991], when anything nuclear seemed to spell doom for humanity and the environment. In 1979, [actors] Jane Fonda and Jack Lemmon produced a frisson of fear with their starring roles in [the movie], "The China Syndrome," a fictional evocation of nuclear disaster in which a reactor meltdown threatens a city's survival. Less than two weeks after the blockbuster film opened, a reactor core meltdown at Pennsylvania's Three Mile Island nuclear power plant sent shivers of very real anguish throughout the country.

What nobody noticed at the time, though, was that Three Mile Island was in fact a success story: The concrete containment structure did just what it was designed to do—prevent radiation from escaping into the environment. And although the reactor itself was crippled, there was no injury or death among nuclear workers or nearby residents. Three Mile Island was the only serious accident in the history of nuclear energy generation in the United States, but it was enough to scare us away from further developing the technology: There hasn't been a nuclear plant ordered up since then.

Today, there are 103 nuclear reactors quietly delivering just 20 percent of America's electricity. Eighty percent of the people living within 10 miles of these plants approve of them (that's not including the nuclear workers). Although I don't live near a nuclear plant, I am now squarely in their camp.

And I am not alone among seasoned environmental activists in changing my mind on this subject. British atmospheric scientist James Lovelock, father of the Gaia theory [ecological theory that living and nonliving parts of the Earth are an integrated, complex system, in which one part affects all], believes that nuclear energy is the only way to avoid catastrophic climate change. Stewart Brand, founder of the "Whole Earth Catalog," says the environmental movement must embrace nuclear energy to wean ourselves from fossil fuels. On occasion, such opinions have been met with excommunication from the anti-nuclear priesthood: The late British Bishop Hugh Montefiore, founder and director of Friends of the Earth, was forced to resign from the group's board after he wrote a pro-nuclear article in a church newsletter.

There are signs of a new willingness to listen, though, even among the staunchest anti-nuclear campaigners. When I attended the Kyoto climate meeting in Montreal [in] December [2005], I spoke to a packed house on the question of a sustainable energy future. I argued that the only way to reduce fossil fuel emissions from electrical production is through an aggressive program of renewable energy sources (hydroelectric, geothermal heat pumps, wind, etc.) plus nuclear. The Greenpeace spokesperson was first at the mike for the question period, and I expected a tongue-lashing. Instead, he began by saying he agreed with much of what I said—not the nuclear bit, of course, but there was a clear feeling that all options must be explored.

Here's why: Wind and solar power have their place, but because they are intermittent and unpredictable they simply can't replace big baseload plants such as coal, nuclear and hydroelectric. Natural gas, a fossil fuel, is too expensive already, and its price is too volatile to risk building big baseload plants. Given that hydroelectric resources are built pretty much to capacity, nuclear is, by elimination, the only viable substitute for coal. It's that simple.

That's not to say that there aren't real problems—as well as various myths—associated with nuclear energy. Each concern deserves careful consideration:

- Nuclear energy is expensive. It is in fact one of the least expensive energy sources. In 2004, the average cost of producing nuclear energy in the United States was less than two cents per kilo-watthour, comparable with coal and hydroelectric. Advances in technology will bring the cost down further in the future.

- Nuclear plants are not safe. Although Three Mile Island was a success story, the accident at Chernobyl [nuclear plant in Ukraine], [in April 1986], was not. But Chernobyl was an accident waiting to happen. This early model of Soviet reactor had no containment vessel, was an inherently bad design and its operators literally blew it up. The multi-agency U.N. Chernobyl Forum reported last year [2005] that 56 deaths could be directly attributed to the accident, most of those from radiation or burns suffered while fighting the fire. Tragic as those deaths were, they pale in comparison to the more than 5,000 coal-mining deaths that occur worldwide every year. No one has died of a radiation-related accident in the history of the U.S. civilian nuclear reactor program. (And although hundreds of uranium mine workers did die from radiation exposure underground in the early years of that industry, that problem was long ago corrected.)

- Nuclear waste will be dangerous for thousands of years. Within 40 years, used fuel has less than one-thousandth of the radioactivity it had when it was removed from the reactor. And it is incorrect to call it waste, because 95 percent of the potential energy is still contained in the used fuel after the first cycle. Now that the United States has removed the ban on recycling used fuel, it will be possible to use that energy and to greatly reduce the amount of waste that needs treatment and disposal. Last month [March 2006], Japan joined France, Britain and Russia in the nuclear-fuel-recycling business. The United States will not be far behind.

- Nuclear reactors are vulnerable to terrorist attack. The six-feet-thick reinforced concrete containment vessel protects the contents from the outside as well as the inside. And even if a jumbo jet did crash into a reactor and breach the containment, the reactor would not explode. There are many types of facilities that are far more vulnerable, including liquid natural gas plants, chemical plants and numerous political targets.

- Nuclear fuel can be diverted to make nuclear weapons. This is the most serious issue associated with nuclear energy and the most difficult to address, as the example of Iran shows. But just because nuclear technology can be put to evil purposes is not an argument to ban its use.

Over the past 20 years, one of the simplest tools—the machete—has been used to kill more than a million people in Africa, far more than were killed in the Hiroshima and Nagasaki [Japan] nuclear bombings [by the United States toward the end of World War II] combined. What are car bombs made of? Diesel oil, fertilizer and cars. If we banned everything that can be used to kill people, we would never have harnessed fire.

The only practical approach to the issue of nuclear weapons proliferation is to put it higher on the international agenda and to use diplomacy and, where necessary, force to prevent countries or terrorists from using nuclear materials for destructive ends. And new technologies such as the [2006] reprocessing system recently introduced in Japan (in which the plutonium is never separated from the uranium) can make it much more difficult for terrorists or rogue states to use civilian materials to manufacture weapons.

The 600-plus coal-fired plants emit nearly 2 billion tons of CO_2 annually—the equivalent of the exhaust from about 300 million automobiles. In addition, the Clean Air Council reports that coal plants are responsible for 64 percent of sulfur dioxide emissions, 26 percent of nitrous oxides and 33 percent of mercury emissions. These pollutants are eroding the health of our environment, producing acid rain, smog, respiratory illness and mercury contamination.

Meanwhile, the 103 nuclear plants operating in the United States effectively avoid the release of 700 million tons of CO_2 emissions annually—the equivalent of the exhaust from more than 100 million automobiles. Imagine if the ratio of coal to nuclear were reversed so that only 20 percent of our electricity was generated from coal and 60 percent from nuclear. This would go a long way toward cleaning the air and reducing greenhouse gas emissions. Every responsible environmentalist should support a move in that direction.

> *"Design studies indicate that existing power generation technologies could capture from 85 to 95 percent of the carbon in coal."*

Clean Coal Technology Is the Future of Energy

David G. Hawkins, Daniel A. Lashof, and Robert H. Williams

In this viewpoint, the authors argue that because coal use is projected well into the future, its pollution potential must be controlled to diminish harmful climate change. They believe a coal energy economy based on carbon capture and sequestration (CCS) is a technological opportunity to meet rising energy demands with a potentially low-cost option. They argue that CCS should be hastened into use through government policy and market incentives. David G. Hawkins is the director of the Climate Center at the Natural Resources Defense Council (NRDC); Daniel A. Lashof is a science director and deputy director of the NRDC's Climate Center, and Robert H. Williams is a senior research scientist at Princeton University.

David G. Hawkins, Daniel A. Lashof, and Robert H. Williams, "What To Do About Coal," *Scientific American*, vol. 295, September 2006, pp. 69–75. Copyright © 2006 by Scientific American, Inc. All rights reserved. Reproduced by permission, www.sciam .com.

As you read, consider the following questions:

1. What process allows coal plant gasification systems to recover carbon dioxide much easier than conventional coal plants, according to the viewpoint?

2. Why is delaying carbon extraction systems at coal power plants short sighted, according to the authors?

3. According to the authors' view, what two policies should be enacted to quickly shift investments to the least pollutant energy technologies?

More than most people realize, dealing with climate change means addressing the problems posed by emissions from coal-fired power plants. Unless humanity takes prompt action to strictly limit the amount of carbon dioxide (CO_2) released into the atmosphere when consuming coal to make electricity, we have little chance of gaining control over global warming.

The Problematic Abundance of Coal

Coal—the fuel that powered the Industrial Revolution [the advent of a mechanized economy, roughly between 1760 and 1830]—is a particularly worrisome source of energy, in part because burning it produces considerably more carbon dioxide per unit of electricity generated than burning either oil or natural gas does. In addition, coal is cheap and will remain abundant long after oil and natural gas have become very scarce. With coal plentiful and inexpensive, its use is burgeoning in the U.S. and elsewhere and is expected to continue rising in areas with abundant coal resources. Indeed, U.S. power providers are expected to build the equivalent of nearly 280 500-megawatt, coal-fired electricity plants between 2003 and 2030. Meanwhile China is already constructing the equivalent of one large coal-fueled power station a week. Over their roughly 60-year life spans, the new generating facilities in operation by 2030 could collectively introduce into the atmosphere about as much carbon dioxide as was released by all the coal burned since the dawn of the Industrial Revolution.

Coal's projected popularity is disturbing not only for those concerned about climate change but also for those worried about other aspects of the environment and about human health and safety. Coal's market price may be low, but the true costs of its extraction, processing and consumption are high. Coal use can lead to a range of harmful consequences, including decapitated mountains, air pollution from acidic and toxic emissions, and water fouled with coal wastes. Extraction also endangers and can kill miners. Together such effects make coal production and conversion to useful energy one of the most destructive activities on the planet.

In keeping with *Scientific American*'s focus on climate concerns in this issue [September 2006], we will concentrate below on methods that can help prevent CO_2 generated during coal conversion from reaching the atmosphere. It goes without saying that the environmental, safety and health effects of coal production and use must be reduced as well. Fortunately, affordable techniques for addressing CO_2 emissions and these other problems already exist, although the will to implement them quickly still lags significantly.

Geologic Storage Strategy

The techniques that power providers could apply to keep most of the carbon dioxide they produce from entering the air are collectively called CO_2 capture and storage (CCS) or geologic carbon sequestration. These procedures involve separating out much of the CO_2 that is created when coal is converted to useful energy and transporting it to sites where it can be stored deep underground in porous media—mainly in depleted oil or gas fields or in saline formations (permeable geologic strata filled with salty water) [see "Can We Bury Global Warming?" by Robert H. Socolow, *Scientific American*, July 2005].

All the technological components needed for CCS at coal conversion plants are commercially ready—having been proved in applications unrelated to climate change mitigation, although integrated systems have not yet been constructed at the necessary scales. Capture technologies have been deployed extensively throughout the world both in the manufacture of chemicals (such as fertilizer) and in the purification of natural gas supplies contaminated with carbon dioxide and hydrogen sulfide ("sour gas"). Industry has gained considerable experience with CO_2 storage in operations that purify natural gas (mainly in Canada) as well as with CO_2 injection to boost oil production (primarily in the U.S.). Enhanced oil recovery processes account for most of the CO_2 that has been sent into underground reservoirs. Currently about 35 million metric tons are injected annually to coax more petroleum out of mature fields, accounting for about 4 percent of U.S. crude oil output.

Implementing CCS at coal-consuming plants is imperative if the carbon dioxide concentration in the atmosphere is to be kept at an acceptable level. The 1992 United Nations Framework Convention on Climate Change calls for stabilizing the atmospheric CO_2 concentration at a "safe" level, but it does not specify what the maximum value should be. The current view of many scientists is that atmospheric CO_2 levels must be kept below 450 parts per million by volume (ppmv) to avoid unacceptable climate changes. Realization of this aggressive goal requires that the power industry start commercial-scale CCS projects within the next few years and expand them rapidly thereafter. This stabilization benchmark cannot be realized by CCS alone but can plausibly be achieved if it is combined with other eco-friendly measures, such as wide improvements in energy efficiency and much expanded use of renewable energy sources.

The Safety of CO_2 Storage

The Intergovernmental Panel on Climate Change (IPCC) estimated in 2005 that is highly probable that geologic media worldwide are capable of sequestering at least two trillion metric tons of CO_2—more than is likely to be produced by fossil-fuel-consuming plants during the 21st century. Society will want to be sure, however, that potential sequestration sites are evaluated carefully for their ability to retain CO_2 before they are allowed to operate. Two classes of risks are of concern: sudden escape and gradual leakage.

Rapid outflow of large amounts of CO_2 could be lethal to those in the vicinity. Dangerous sudden releases—such as that which occurred in 1986 at Lake Nyos in Cameroon, when CO_2 of volcanic origin asphyxiated 1,700 nearby villagers and thousands of cattle—are improbable for engineered CO_2 storage projects in carefully selected, deep porous geologic formations, according to the IPCC.

Gradual seepage of carbon dioxide into the air is also an issue, because over time it could defeat the goal of CCS. The 2005 IPCC report estimated that the fraction retained in appropriately selected and managed geologic reservoirs is very likely to exceed 99 percent over 100 years and likely to exceed 99 percent over 1,000 years. What remains to be demonstrated is whether in practice operators can routinely keep CO_2 leaks to levels that avoid unacceptable environmental and public health risks.

Technology Choices

Design studies indicate that existing power generation technologies could capture from 85 to 95 percent of the carbon in coal as CO_2, with the rest released to the atmosphere.

The coal conversion technologies that come to dominate will be those that can meet the objectives of climate change mitigation at the least cost. Fundamentally different approaches to CCS would be pursued for power plants using the conventional pulverized-coal steam cycle and the newer integrated gasification combined cycle (IGCC). Although today's coal IGCC power (with CO_2 venting) is slightly more expensive than coal steam-electric power, it looks like IGCC is the most effective and least expensive option for CCS.

Standard plants burn coal in a boiler at atmospheric pressure. The heat generated in coal combustion transforms water into steam, which turns a steam turbine, whose mechanical energy is converted to electricity by a generator. In modern plants the gases produced by combustion (flue gases) then pass through devices that remove particulates and oxides of sulfur and nitrogen before being exhausted via smokestacks into the air.

Carbon dioxide could be extracted from the flue gases of such steam-electric plants after the removal of conventional pollutants. Because the flue gases contain substantial amounts of nitrogen (the result of burning coal in air, which is about 80 percent nitrogen), the carbon dioxide would be recovered at low concentration and pressure—which implies that the CO_2 would have to be removed from large volumes of gas using processes that are both energy-intensive and expensive. The captured CO_2 would then be compressed and piped to an appropriate storage site.

In an IGCC system coal is not burned but rather partially oxidized (reacted with limited quantities of oxygen from an air separation plant, and with steam) at high pressure in a gasifier. The product of gasification is so-called synthesis gas, or syngas, which is composed mostly of carbon monoxide and hydrogen, undiluted with nitrogen. In current practice, IGCC operations remove most conventional pollutants from the syngas and then burn it to turn both gas and steam turbine-generators in what is called a combined cycle.

In an IGCC plant designed to capture CO_2, the syngas exiting the gasifier, after being cooled and cleaned of particles, would be reacted with steam to produce a gaseous mixture made up mainly of carbon dioxide and hydrogen. The CO_2 would then be extracted, dried, compressed and transported

Clean Coal Technology

Clean Coal Technology describes a category of technologies that allow for the use of coal to generate electricity while meeting environmental regulations at low cost.

• In the short term, the goal of the program is to meet existing and emerging environmental regulations, which will dramatically reduce compliance costs for controlled mercury, NOx, SO_2, and fine particulate at new and existing coal power plants.

• In the mid-term, the goal of the program is to develop low-cost, super clean coal power plants, with efficiencies 50 per cent higher than today's average. The higher efficiencies will reduce emissions at minimal costs.

• In the long term, the goal of the program is to develop low-cost, zero emission power plants with efficiencies close to double that of today's fleet.

National Energy Policy Development Group, "Reliable, Affordable, and Environmentally Sound Energy for America's Future." 2001, www.whitehouse.gov.

to a storage site. The remaining hydrogen-rich gas would be burned in a combined cycle plant to generate power

The Economics of CCS

Analyses indicate that carbon dioxide capture at IGCC plants consuming high-quality bituminous coals [a medium-soft coal, the most common and useful of U.S.-mined coals, as it is used to produce energy and coke making for the steel industries] would entail significantly smaller energy and cost penalties and lower total generation costs than what could be achieved in conventional coal plants that captured and stored CO_2. Gasification systems recover CO_2 from a gaseous stream at high concentration and pressure, a feature that makes the process much easier than it would be in conventional steam facilities. (The extent of the benefits is less clear for lower-grade subbituminous coals and lignite [the softest classification of coal with the highest moisture content and poorer fuel efficiency compared to harder coal], which have received much less study.) Precombustion removal of conventional pollutants, including mercury, makes it feasible to realize very low levels of emissions at much reduced costs and with much smaller energy penalties than with cleanup systems for flue gases in conventional plants.

Captured carbon dioxide can be transported by pipeline up to several hundred kilometers to suitable geologic storage sites and subsequent subterranean storage with the pressure produced during capture. Longer distances may, however, require recompression to compensate for friction losses during pipeline transfer.

Overall, pursuing CCS for coal power facilities requires the consumption of more coal to generate a kilowatt-hour of electricity than when CO_2 is vented—about 30 percent extra in the case of coal steam-electric plants and less than 20 percent more for IGCC plants. But overall coal use would not necessarily increase, because the higher price of coal-based electricity resulting from adding CCS equipment would dampen demand for coal-based electricity, making renewable energy sources and energy-efficient products more desirable to consumers.

The cost of CCS will depend on the type of power plant, the distance to the storage site, the properties of the storage reservoir and the availability of opportunities (such as enhanced oil recovery) for selling the captured CO_2. A recent study co-authored by one of us (Williams) estimated the incremental electric generation costs of two alternative CCS options for coal IGCC plants under typical production, transport and storage conditions. For CO_2 sequestration in a saline formation 100 kilometers from a power plant, the study calculated that the incremental cost of CCS would be 1.9 cents per kilowatt-hour (beyond the generation cost of 4.7 cents per kilowatt-hour for a coal IGCC plant that vents CO_2—a 40 percent premium). For CCS pursued in conjunction with enhanced oil recovery at a distance of 100 kilometers from the conversion plant, the analysis finds no increase in net generation cost would occur as long as the oil price is at least $35 per barrel, which is much lower than current [2006] prices.

CCS Now or Later?

Many electricity producers in the industrial world recognize that environmental concerns will at some point force them to implement CCS if they are to continue to employ coal. But rather than building plants that actually capture and store carbon dioxide, most plan to construct conventional steam facilities they claim will be "CO_2 capture ready"—convertible when CCS is mandated.

Power providers often defend those decisions by noting that the U.S. and most other countries with coal-intensive energy economies have not yet instituted policies for climate change mitigation that would make CCS cost-effective for uses not associated with enhanced oil recovery. Absent revenues from sales to oil field operators, applying CCS to new coal plants using current technology would be the least-cost path only if the cost of emitting CO_2 were at least $25 to $30 per metric ton. Many current policy proposals for climate change mitigation in the U.S. envision significantly lower cost penalties to power providers for releasing CO_2 (or similarly, payments for CO_2 emissions-reduction credits).

Yet delaying CCS at coal power plants until economy-wide carbon dioxide control costs are greater than CCS costs is shortsighted. For several reasons, the coal and power industries and society would ultimately benefit if deployment of plants fitted with CCS equipment were begun now.

First, the fastest way to reduce CCS costs is via "learning by doing"—the accumulation of experience in building and running such plants. The faster the understanding is accumulated, the quicker the know-how with the new technology will grow, and the more rapidly the costs will drop.

Second, installing CCS equipment as soon as possible should save money in the long run. Most power stations currently under construction will still be operating decades from now, when it is likely that CCS efforts will be obligatory. Retrofitting generating facilities for CCS is inherently more expensive than deploying CCS in new plants. Moreover, in the absence of CO_2 emission limits, familiar conventional coal steam-electric technologies will tend to be favored for most new plant construction over newer gasification technologies, for which CCS is more cost-effective.

Low Cost Move to Energy Alternatives

Finally, rapid implementation would allow for continued use of fossil fuels in the near term (until more environmentally friendly sources become prevalent) without pushing atmospheric carbon dioxide beyond tolerable levels. Our studies indicate that it is feasible to stabilize atmospheric CO_2 levels at 450 ppmv over the next half a century if coal-based energy is completely decarbonized and other measures. . . are implemented. This effort would involve decarbonizing 36 gigawatts [10^9 watts of power] of new coal generating capacity by 2020 (corresponding to 7 percent of the new coal capacity expected to be built worldwide during the decade beginning in 2011 under business-as-usual conditions). In the 35 years after 2020, CO_2 capture would need to rise at an average rate of about 12 percent a year. Such a sustained pace is high compared with typical market growth rates for energy but is not unprecedented. It is much less than the expansion rate for nuclear generating capacity in its heyday—1956 to 1980— during which global capacity rose at an average rate of 40 percent annually. Further, the expansion rates for both wind and solar photovoltaic power capacities worldwide have hovered around 30 percent a year since the early 1990s. In all three cases, such growth would not have been practical without public policy measures to support them.

Our calculations indicate that the costs of CCS deployment would be manageable as well. Using conservative assumptions—such as that technology will not improve over time—we estimate that the present worth of the cost of capturing and storing all CO_2 produced by coal-based electricity generation plants during the next 200 years will be $1.8 trillion (in 2002 dollars). That might seem like a high price tag, but it is equivalent to just 0.07 percent of the current value [as of 2006] of gross world product over the same interval. Thus, it is plausible that a rapid decarbonization path for coal is both physically and economically feasible, although detailed regional analyses are needed to confirm this conclusion.

Policy Push Is Needed

Those good reasons for commencing concerted CCS efforts soon will probably not move the industry unless it is also prodded by new public policies. Such initiatives would be part of a broader drive to control carbon dioxide emissions from all sources.

In the U.S., a national program to limit CO_2 emissions must be enacted soon to introduce the government regulations and market incentives necessary to shift investment to the least-polluting energy technologies promptly and on a wide scale. Leaders in the American business and policy communities increasingly agree that quantifiable and enforceable restrictions on global warming emissions are imperative and inevitable. To ensure that power companies put into practice the reductions in a cost-effective fashion, a market for trading CO_2 emissions credits should be created—one similar to that for the sulfur emissions that cause acid rain. In such a plan, organizations that intend to exceed designated emission limits may buy credits from others that are able to stay below these values.

Enhancing energy efficiency efforts and raising renewable energy production are critical to achieving carbon dioxide limits at the lowest possible cost. A portion of the emission allowances created by a carbon cap-and-trade program should be allocated to the establishment of a fund to help overcome institutional barriers and technical risks that obstruct widespread deployment of otherwise cost-effective CO_2 mitigation technologies.

Even if a carbon dioxide cap-and-trade program were enacted in the next few years the economic value of CO_2 emissions reduction may not be enough initially to convince power providers to invest in power systems with CCS. To avoid the construction of another generation of conventional coal plants, it is essential that the federal government establish incentives that promote CCS.

One approach would be to insist that an increasing share of total coal-based electricity generation comes from facilities that meet a low CO_2 emissions standard—perhaps a maximum of 30 grams of carbon per kilowatt-hour (an achievable goal using today's coal CCS technologies). Such a goal might be achieved by obliging electricity producers that use coal to include a growing fraction of decarbonized coal power in their supply portfolios. Each covered electricity producer could either generate the required amount of decarbonized coal power or purchase decarbonized generation credits. This system would share the incremental costs of CCS for coal power among all U.S. coal-based electricity producers and consumers.

If the surge of conventional coal-fired power plants currently on drawing boards is built as planned [as of 2006], atmospheric carbon dioxide levels will almost certainly exceed 450 ppmv [parts per million volume]. We can meet global

73

needs while still stabilizing CO_2 at 450 ppmv, however, through a combination of improved efficiency in energy use, greater reliance on renewable energy resources and, for the new coal investments that are made, the installation of CO_2 capture and geologic storage technologies. Even though there is no such thing as "clean coal," more can and must be done to reduce the dangers and environmental degradations associated with coal production and use. An integrated low-carbon energy strategy that incorporates CO_2 capture and storage can reconcile substantial use of coal in the coming decades with the imperative to prevent catastrophic changes to the earth's climate.

> *"In a deregulated world, sweeping changes like carbon limits or pollution controls or rules governing the uses of power-plant technology can come only from government intervention, from intense regulation."*

Clean Coal Technologies Are Not the Future of Energy

S.C. Gwynne

S. C. Gwynne uses the example of Texas' future energy choices as indicative of the national energy debate about coal and climate change. Energy Corporation TXU proposed building eleven new coal-fired electrical generators in the state. The debate following the proposal is revealing. Gwynne argues that the secret to future energy is not an energy source, like coal, but within the problematic area of energy deregulation. S.C. Gwynne is an executive editor at Texas Monthly *and author of* The Outlaw Bank: A Wild Ride into the Secret Heart of BCCI.

As you read, consider the following questions:

1. According to Gwynne there are no inconsequential energy decisions. Why?

S.C. Gwynne, "Coal Hard Facts," *Texas Monthly*, January 2007. Reproduced by permission.-

2. Why does Gwynne think it is ironic that coal has re-emerged as the fuel choice of electric power companies in 2007?

3. What are U.S. geopolitical reasons for recommitting to coal, according to the viewpoint?

4. How does deregulation, according to the viewpoint, prevent TXU Corporation from using IGCC coal-burning technology to reduce carbon emissions?

When you turn on your television set, air conditioner, or dishwasher, you are doing something that is at once mechanical and moral. The mechanical part stems from your rudimentary demand for electrons: You push a button, and somewhere in Texas a huge turbine throttles up, spins a magnet inside a coil, and initiates a massive electron-bumping chain reaction that travels in light-speed waves through miles of transmission lines to reach the circuits in your house. The moral complexity lies in the choices implicit in that action. In order to power your appliances, you must summon electricity from a vast sea of energy, a largely sealed electrical grid that stops at the Texas border. Generating plants across the state, powered variously by coal, gas, nuclear fission, wind, and water, dump electrical current into this grid, and by throwing a switch you engage them all. No matter what your politics are, how much of an environmentalist or conservationist you might be, or whether you actually give a damn where your electricity comes from, you're complicit in every energy policy decision the state of Texas has made for the past fifty years.

No Easy Energy Choices

And there are no inconsequential energy decisions. Coal and gas are relatively cheap but pollute the air and contribute to global warming; nuclear power does not pollute the air but creates radioactive waste that will be simmering in containment pits for thousands of years; hydropower is clean but requires the damming of rivers and the destruction of habitat; wind and solar are gentle but expensive, and electrical expense is a leading cause of eviction for poor people in America. In Texas's grid, 91 percent of the power comes from coal and gas. That means that when you goose your air conditioner a few degrees, you are electing, de facto, to hasten global warming and add to the air you will breathe small but ineradicable amounts of sulfur dioxide, nitrogen oxide, and mercury.

If this seems a bit dramatic, it is nonetheless empirically true, and it may explain the loud, organized protest that has erupted in the past few months [of 2007] over proposals to build seventeen giant new coal-fired power plants in Texas. The key word there is "coal." Historically the dirtiest energy source, coal has been completely out of fashion for 25 years. When ground to dust and burned, it emits harmful chemicals, including fine particulate matter that causes asthma. Facilities that use it also burp forth large volumes of carbon dioxide, which is harmless to humans (it's the fizz in Coke), but is the leading cause of global warming. Together, the seventeen proposed plants would more than double Texas's reliance on this problematic fossil fuel.

The push to build the plants is being led by the Dallas-based former monopoly TXU, which last April [2006] announced a five-year plan to put eleven of them online at a cost of $10 billion, the most ambitious such project anywhere in the country.

The Oversized Return of Coal

The reemergence of coal is, in the history of electricity generation, an astounding turn of events. After a quarter-century slumber, during which it had clear status as yesterday's technology, coal is once again the fuel of choice for electric power. One hundred fifty-four coal-fired power plants are currently on drawing boards in the United States [as of 2007]. Three years ago there were none. Globally, some one thousand new coal plants have been proposed. That this is taking place just as global warming is gaining popular acceptance is one of the great environmental ironies of the twenty-first century. Coal is by far the most carbon-intensive fuel—emitting twice the carbon dioxide per unit of energy that natural gas does. The weird climatic changes you've read about—the melting polar ice cap, the retreating glaciers in China, islands vanishing in the Pacific, droughts in Africa, killer hurricanes in the Gulf of Mexico—are all directly related to how much carbon dioxide we put into the atmosphere. In their working lifetimes, about 35 years, those one thousand proposed plants would spew more carbon dioxide than was emitted by man-made sources on the entire planet from 1750 to 2000.

Throughout most of the twentieth century, coal was America's fuel of choice. Nuclear power, which now accounts for 20 percent of our electricity, bid briefly to replace it as the dominant technology in the sixties and seventies but ran into a political wall after the 1979 partial core meltdown at Three Mile Island, in Pennsylvania. Nuke plants are also grotesquely difficult to get permitted and freakishly expensive to build, and there is still no long-term solution to the problem of how and where to store the radioactive waste they generate. Even if a solution is found, it will likely be 2020 before we see any new nuclear plants in operation. What moved America away from coal was the arrival of cheap natural gas. Starting in the [President Ronald] Reagan era, gas was so inexpensive, and so much cleaner to burn than coal, that the choice was obvious. From 1980 to the present, almost all the power-generating plants that were built in Texas and in the United States were fired by natural gas.

Those days are over. Gas is up 300 percent since 1999. It is now three times as expensive as coal and projected to stay costly well into the twenty-first century. In a country that is rapidly deregulating its electric utilities—23 states plus the District of Columbia now let energy companies compete for

Deregulation Is Risky Business

The purchase of KeySpan by the British energy giant National Grid PLC is only the latest in a wave of mergers and consolidations of deregulated gas and electric utilities. While the new system of free-market utilities is supposed to be good for consumers, public utility deregulation has been mainly an invitation to price-gouging and greater risks to the system's reliability.

Robert Kuttner, "Deregulation Hasn't Worked,"
Boston Globe, *March 4, 2006.*

consumers' business—holding down the cost of power is the key to success. Add a White House that is coal friendly, the technology to cut emissions of pollutants (but not carbon dioxide) by 90 percent, a nuclear industry still paralyzed by its inability to dispose of its waste, the impracticality of wind and solar in handling bulk demand for power, and a virtual moratorium on new plant construction for the past ten years, and you have the sort of economic and regulatory perfect storm that produces 154 new coal plants.

Coal Geopolitics

In the United States, there are also strategic, geopolitical reasons for recommitting to coal. If you think the Middle East has a lot of oil, consider this: There is more energy under Illinois than in all of the proven and potential oil reserves of Saudi Arabia. We own 25 percent of the world's recoverable coal. That amounts to 250 years of energy security. If the rest of the world were to shut us off from its oil and gas, we could run almost everything in our gigantic economy on domestic coal. We could convert our coal to diesel fuel for our cars and trucks, as the Third Reich [of Nazi Germany] did, and it would still take more than two centuries for us to run through it. Coal is immediately available, easy to extract, and not subject to the whims of foreign markets or foreign dictators. In a post—September 11 world, these things matter.

Today, coal accounts for 52 percent of our power, almost all of which comes from technological dinosaurs built in the fifties, sixties, and seventies. They produce the overwhelming majority of the power-plant pollution in this country. A new generation of coal plants is coming. The only question is what it will took like. . . .

Gasified Coal: Future or Fact?

That better way goes by the name of integrated gasification combined cycle. Get used to the term, and its acronym, IGCC. You are going to be hearing it a lot in years to come. For environmentalists, it has become something of a mantra. Any new coal-fueled plants, they say, should be built with IGCC. And a number of power companies agree. Despite the considerably greater expense of building with IGCC—some $200 million or more per plant—6.5 percent of the coal plants now being proposed in America will use that technology. Several major utilities, including American Electric Power, the largest utility in the country, with the largest fleet of coal plants, have stated that IGCC is now their future technology of choice for burning coal.

The advantage of gasified coal comes in the sequence of emissions controls. Unlike pulverized coal, which requires a chemical plant on the back end of the factory to remove pollutants, gasified coal allows acidic and particulate components to be removed before they are burned, thus keeping them out of the stack and reducing the cost and difficulty of their removal. After that, the process is in many ways the same. The synthetic gas feeds a combustion turbine, whose exhaust heat is then reused to drive a steam turbine. IGCC is indeed a cleaner way to burn coal, though advancements in pulverized-coal technology have rendered the IGCC advantage modest in terms of local air pollution. According to numbers from the Environmental Protection Agency, a new and improved pulverized plant burning Powder River Basin coal (a fairly clean coal mined in Wyoming that TXU plans to use in all but one of its new facilities) would achieve a 90 percent reduction in sulfur dioxide emissions compared with an average U.S. coal plant, such as Big Brown [in Texas], in 2004; IGCC does only a little bit better, achieving a 93 percent reduction. Both achieve the same 83 percent decrease in nitrogen oxide. The major difference between IGCC and pulverized-coal systems is that the former provides a much easier and cheaper way of taking carbon dioxide out of the stack.

But IGCC is an expensive, commercially unproven technology, and according to TXU, it does not perform well with the Western coal used in Texas. Eastern coal, from West Virginia, Ohio, and other states, has a higher BTU [British therman unit] value and more moisture and performs better with the gasification process. "We cannot make it work with the coal that is available here," says Michael McCall, the chairman and CEO of TXU's wholesale division. Why can't the plants use Eastern coal? That's logistically impossible, TXU maintains. Since each plant consumes 140 train cars of coal per day, 1,400 such cars would have to make the trip from West Virginia to Texas every 24 hours. . . .

The fact is that IGCC's ability to deliver the environmentalists' claims is far from guaranteed. It is still a developing technology with few working models anywhere in the world. There are only two IGCC plants in the United States (in Florida and Indiana), both set up as demonstration facilities by the U.S. Department of Energy and partly subsidized by the government. Plagued by technical troubles, they have had a mixed record of success. Like TXU, most power companies regard these results with skepticism. Seventy-nine percent of the coal plants currently being proposed in America will use pulverized coal (another 15 percent will use a coal-burning technology called circulating fluidized bed). The first private IGCC plant will likely belong to AEP, which has contracted with GE Energy and Bechtel to produce two big, 630-megawatt gasification facilities in Ohio and West Virginia. Construction on the two has not yet begun. They are years from operation. . . .

The Low-Cost Option in Deregulation

In the days before competition, TXU, like other regulated electric monopolies, was never really at risk when it built a plant. It would simply secure guarantees from the public utility commission that it would be able to charge its customers enough to recoup its capital costs. But as of January 1, 2007, the Texas electricity market is, for all practical purposes, fully price competitive, which means that any losses incurred by TXU are its own problem. TXU must be able to match or beat its competitors' prices, so unless the state or federal government mandates radically lower emissions for everyone, [TXU CEO John] Wilder is going to take the lowest cost option available. During our interview, he proposed, quite seriously, to build an IGCC plant in the Dallas–Fort Worth area today. But only if the cities take the risk. In a free market, he says, he can't afford to take it himself. "If we were a regulated monopoly, we would probably be arguing for IGCC," Wilder told me. "The customer eats the expense. But that is not the world we compete in."

The world he competes in does, however, contain a number of powerful politicians who support taxes on carbon emissions (including potential presidential candidates Hillary Clinton and John McCain). Since its new plants will pump 78 million tons of carbon dioxide into the atmosphere annually—in addition to the 55 million tons it currently emits—this poses a significant commercial risk to TXU's business plan. California recently initiated laws mandating carbon dioxide reduction that take effect in 2020. When asked if he expects to have to deal with such legislation, Wilder acknowledged that the future would likely be a "carbon-constrained world" but added, "We think we have a good view of how those rules might unfold."

Energy Is Local

In spite of all the talk about carbon dioxide, the bedrock issue here is still entirely local: air quality in Texas cities, especially smog-causing chemicals that may make it difficult for Houston, Dallas—Fort Worth, and other cities to meet increasingly strict federal clean-air standards. Though TXU's plan represents a 20 percent reduction in average pollution across the entire region, on certain days and with certain wind conditions, individual areas may be worse off. "People don't breathe average air," says Jim Marston, the executive director of Environmental Defense. "They breathe the air that they breathe." Adds his colleague Ramon Alvarez: "There are more offsets from old plants in northeast Texas, more new emissions in south central Texas, so that in certain areas, improving the average isn't going to mean anything."

Perhaps the best example of this is TXU's mammoth new two-boiler plant proposed at Oak Grove, near the town of Franklin, just north of College Station. Unlike the rest of the TXU plants, which will run on Powder River Basin coal, Oak Grove will burn lignite [the softest coal type, with the highest moisture content]. The plant will run through 2.5 million pounds of it each hour, emitting vast amounts of pollutants that were not in this area before: 1,446 pounds of mercury and as much nitrogen oxide as from the exhaust of 470,000 automobiles. On its first day of operation, the plant will be the fourth-largest emitter of mercury in the country; however, when averaged with TXU's proposed coat fleet, it is part of the 20 percent overall reduction in pollutants.

The local residents don't see it that way. Some have banded, together to form Our Land, Our Lives, a group whose goal is to stop the Oak Grove plant. They have signed petitions and taken out ads in newspapers and filed a federal lawsuit claiming that TXU's permit application violates the federal Clean Air Act. They have also had a stunning bit of recent success. After they contested TXU's permit application, an administrative law judge in Austin ruled in August that the Oak Grove plant "failed to prove by a preponderance of the evidence that its proposed source would not cause or contribute to a condition of air pollution." Such a ruling does not carry the force of law; it constitutes merely a "recommendation" to the TCEQ [Texas Commission on Environment Quality]. Virtually no one interviewed for this story, on either side, believed that the TCEQ would deny the application, and in fact, following the ruling, TCEQ executive director Glenn Shankle wrote a detailed response arguing on TXU's behalf. Still, it showed that there may be legal obstacles ahead for TXU in its quest for approval.

This same notion of "local" versus "average" pollution can be applied to Dallas–Fort Worth and other cities in the region. While the TERC study did state that, based on average air quality, TXU's proposed plants would reduce the overall pollution in Dallas–Fort Worth, the report also said, partly in contradiction to itself: "The ozone impacts of the proposed new EGUs [electric generating units] tend to be geographically separated from the benefits of TXU's offset strategy. This is because many of the new EGUs are in Central Texas whereas many of TXU's offset emissions reductions occur in Northeast Texas. . . . The net impact on DFW [Dallas-Fort Worth] . . . depends upon the relative frequency of high ozone days with southeast winds (from Central Texas) versus east winds (from Northeast Texas)."

A Radical Experiment or Dark Future

The point may be a technical one, but on it hangs a good deal of the case against TXU's plan. At issue is whether Dallas–Fort

Worth is in compliance with federal clean-air standards. Right now it is not, and unless it improves, it will soon face penalties—denial of industrial permits and road building funds, difficulty in attracting new industries, and so forth. Compliance is measured by air quality on four selected days. On some days, certain spots will be much more polluted than others. "It's the difference between meeting the rule or not being subject to sanctions and having to do a bunch of offsets," says Marston. "We think this will make it almost impossible for Dallas–Fort Worth to reach attainment." That could mean hundreds of millions of dollars in lost annual revenues and resources, according to Laura Miller and the Texas Clean Air Cities Coalition. "We have only eighteen plants now, which have helped Dallas–Fort Worth and Houston fall out of compliance with federal environmental laws," Miller wrote in an August 21 [2006] opinion column in the *Dallas Morning News.* "What's the point of cities screwing in low-wattage bulbs and buying natural gas-fueled police cars if you've got soot from seventeen new coal plants billowing your way?" . . .

What the fight over these coal plants suggests, however, is that some people may very well decide that they prefer the good old days when the public utility commissions told companies like TXU how much they would charge and the types of plants they would build. California, Arizona, and other states have deregulated only to decide later that they wanted to "reregulate." Texas is thus far the most radical national experiment in free-market competition in the electric power business. It is possible that legislators may try to rein it back in. And it is entirely possible, too, that some of the anti-TXU lawsuits may bear fruit. One of them, filed by Environmental Defense, claims that the state is breaking its own laws by refusing to make TXU and other companies consider IGCC technology.

In the meantime, there is little reason to expect that TXU is going to behave differently than it does today. Blaming TXU for proposing its plants is a lot like blaming General Motors for building Suburbans [SUVs]. The two companies are acting fully in accordance with who they are and with what their goals are. They are both obeying government rules and selling products in a free marketplace. Like the environmental lobby, their behavior is virtually encoded at this point. In a deregulated world, sweeping changes like carbon limits or pollution controls or rules governing the uses of power-plant technology can come only from government intervention, from intense regulation. And that was what Texas legislators worked for most of the nineties to get rid of. We will soon see if they have second thoughts.

Periodical Bibliography

The following articles have been selected to supplement the diverse views presented in this chapter.

Mark Bryden and Doug McCorkle	"Virtual Engineering: In Powerful New Workspaces, the Next-Generation Power Plant Is Only the Beginning," *Mechanical Engineer*, November 2005, www.memagazine.com.
BusinessWeek	"In Asia, A Hot Market for Carbon," December 12, 2005, www.businessweek.com.
Steve Fiscor	"Environmentalists Soften Their Stance," *Coal Age*, 2006, vol. 111, no. 4, www.coalage.com.
Thomas Friedman	"My Favorite Green Lump," *New York Times*, January 10, 2007, www.nytimes.com.
Larry Metzroth	"Can U.S. Coal Meet Projected Demand?" *Power Engineering*, July 2006, www.pepei.pen net.com.
Process Engineering	"Industry Focus—Energy Efficiency: Coal Key to Future Power Supply," *Process Engineering*, June 28, 2006, www.processengineering.co.uk.
Roanoke Times	"Webb Pushes Effort to Clean Emissions: Carbon Sequestration Could Clear Way for Wide Use of Coal and Related Technologies," *Roanoke Times*, March 20, 2007, www.roanoke.com.
Matthew L. Wald	"The Search for New Oil Sources Leads to Processed Coal," *New York Times*, July 5, 2006, www.nytimes.com.
Emma Young	"Going Underground," *New Scientist*, September 3, 2005, www.newscientist.com.
Gregory Zuckerman	"High-Sulfur Coal Has Investors Glowing," *Wall Street Journal*, April 24, 2006, www.wsj.com.

CHAPTER 2

Is Coal Use Justified?

Chapter Preface

The energy future is coming—and it is not coal or any other fossil fuel that will drive the world's economy, according to futurist and author, Ray Kurzweil. Kurzweil is an inventor, notably credited for his work on virtual reality, speech and character recognition, and author of several books, including *The Age of Intelligent Machines*.

Kurzweil says to forget arguments whether coal is the energy future. According to Kurzweil's way of thinking, debate over coal, hydrogen or nuclear energies is irrelevant. His logic? The sun. Kurzweil believes we can capture sunlight entering the Earth's atmosphere and use it to meet our global energy needs without any fossil fuels and their greenhouse gas emissions. Kurzweil thinks global warming would be a problem if industrial emissions continued at their current level for hundreds of years, or if they sharply escalated. He thinks that will not happen. The reason is nanotechnology.

Nanotechnology is an emerging technology using various scientific and engineering disciplines to manipulate and create functional systems at the molecular-sized level. In other words, systems that operate on a scale so small they can only be viewed by high-powered microscopes. The promises of nanotechnology are many. The U.S. National Science Foundation describes two: "Imagine a medical device that travels through the human body to seek out and destroy small clusters of cancerous cells before they can spread . . . or materials much lighter than steel that possess ten times as much strength." As of this writing, billions of dollars are invested in nanotechnology research.

In June 2006, Kurzweil answered online questions posed to him through the *Washington Post*'s "Beyond the Future" series of live Web chats. Kurzweil answered a question about the ecology of energy like this:

If we captured 1% of 1% of the sunlight (1 part in 10,000) we could meet 100% of our energy needs without ANY fossil fuels. We can't do that today (in 2006) because the solar panels are too heavy, expensive, and inefficient. But there are new nanoengineereed designs that are much more effective. Within five to six years, this technology will make a significant contribution. Within 20 years, it can provide all of our energy needs. The discussions talk about current trends continuing for the next century as if nothing is going to change. I think global warming is real but it has been modest thus far—one degree f (Fahrenheit) in 100 years. It would concern [me] if that continued or accelerated for a long period of time, but that's not going to happen. And it's not just environmental concern that will drive this; the $2 trillion we spend on energy is providing plenty of economic incentive. I don't see any disasters occurring in the next 10 years from this.

If Kurzweil is correct, we are basing energy-economic policy on past ideas that incrementally fix old systems. Our energy logic, as of this writing, makes energy fixes more complicated by trying to remedy old sources of power. For instance, rather than trying to clean up coal emissions through innovation, why not use other technology to erase the problem? We do not need energy plants if we think like Kurzweil; the sun is the largest energy plant we will ever need. According to Kurzweil, advances in nanotechnology will link us to cleaner energy, bypassing old logic, such as material extraction and emissions, in the process.

If Kurzweil is even partially correct, the environmental destruction that some of the viewpoints in the following chapter describe visited upon regions where coal is harvested is cruel and unjustified. Many world leaders and energy experts would argue, as you will also read in this chapter, that claims such as Kurzweil's are impractical for the world we live in. The authors of the following viewpoints discuss and argue whether coal use, under a wide range of scenarios and impacts, is justified.

"One alternative to burning coal directly is to first convert coal into something called Dimethyl ether. (DME) . . . DME is non-toxic and environmentally friendly."

Transforming Coal into Alternative Fuels Justifies Its Use

Michael Shedlock

In this viewpoint, Michael Shedlock argues that China's economic and environmental concerns about coal are synonymous with the world. Although many commentators express dismay at China's potential to exacerbate global warming, Shedlock writes that the Chinese are invested in transforming it from dirty energy into a clean form. Shedlock argues coal use is justified by the practical needs of oversized economies such as in China and by environmental innovation that will transform the industry. Michael Shedlock is an investment representative for SitkaPacific Capital Management and coeditor of the stock market and economic advisory publication, Whiskey & Gunpowder.

Michael Shedlock, "How Black Is Coal?" *MISH's Global Economic Trend Analysis*, August 30, 2006, http://globaleconomicanalysis.blogspot.com. Reproduced by permission.

As you read, consider the following questions:

1. Michael Shedlock argues in the viewpoint that there is an alternative to the pessimism of Jeff Goodell's book *Big Coal*. What is it?

2. According to the viewpoint, due to coal shortages, China will only build large-scale coal-to-DME plants. Why does this seeming contradiction make sense, according to Shedlock?

3. How will China gauge the success of its coal-to-DME program, according to the viewpoint?

In a review of the book "Big Coal" *The Rocky Mountain News* is reporting on the black side of coal dependency.

> America is the Saudi Arabia of coal. Whereas Saudi Arabia has more than 20 percent of the world's oil reserves, the United States has more than 25 percent of the world's recoverable coal reserves—approximately 270 billion tons.
>
> Russia comes in a distant second with 176 billion tons; China has 126 billion tons, and Europe has a paltry 36 billion tons. It's no surprise that many in America's coal industry are making a strong push for our increased reliance on coal.

The Extraction-Emission Problem

> Jeff Goodell [the author of *Big Coal*], however, isn't so optimistic. While he agrees absolutely that America's coal reserves provide a solid natural resource base that ensures our long-term energy needs, providing for those needs with coal will be problematic.
>
> First, extracting coal is extremely destructive—oil can be pumped out of the ground from a few relatively small holes, and is easier to store and transport. But getting at coal requires extensive underground mining, or, worse, strip min-

ing. Entire Appalachian mountains have been torn down to get at the coal underneath, and at Wyoming's massive strip mines, according to one saying, "they don't really mine coal, they just move dirt." Because it is a solid, coal is far more expensive and difficult to transport than oil.

Second, burning coal introduces vast amounts of CO_2 [carbon dioxide] into the atmosphere, continuing the cycle of global warming and increasing the likelihood of more frequent and more devastating disasters like [the 2005] hurricane Katrina [that was catastrophic for the U.S. Gulf Coast region].

Third, reliance on coal, like other fossil fuels, discourages us from searching for alternative fuel sources. And finally, coal mining has a significant human cost—something Goodell is keenly aware of: "Coal is the only energy source that requires workers to put their lives on the line on a daily basis."

Is the Black Side of Coal Really That Black?

The answer of course is another question "compared to what?"

Like everything else related to energy, the answers are seldom black and white but rather shades of grey. One alternative to burning coal directly is to first convert coal into something called Dimethyl ether (DME). DME, is a colorless water soluble gas. DME is non-toxic and environmentally friendly. It can also be used for transportation. A September 2004 research paper by Princeton University entitled "Transportation Fuel from Coal with Low CO_2 Emissions" discusses the possibilities.

> This paper explores a strategy for mitigating climate change for coal-derived synthetic fuels both by CCS [carbon capture and sequestration] and by choosing an energy carrier that facilitates a shift to more-efficient energy end-use technology. The focus is on dimethyl ether (DME). Its high cetane number [measure of the combustion quality of diesel fuel, determining overall diesel fuel quality] makes DME a

suitable candidate fuel for compression ignition engine vehicles, which are more energy efficient than spark-ignition engine vehicles. Compression ignition engine vehicles are not more widely used in part because of difficulties in realizing simultaneously low levels of emissions of both NOx [nitrogen oxide] and particulate matter (PM), which are being sought in tightening air pollutant emission regulations through-out the world, driven by public health concerns. The tradeoffs that make simultaneous NOx and PM control difficult for diesel fuel do not exist for DME, the combustion of which generates essentially no PM because of the absence of C-C bonds [carbon-carbon bond: by sharing electrons a bond between two carbon atoms is formed] and of sulfur. These pollution control advantages can facilitate a transition to fuel-efficient vehicles such as compression ignition engine/hybrid electric vehicles, [fuel ignites by injection into a combustion chamber compressed to high temperatures; used in diesel engines] although the pollution control advantages offered by DME are offset in part by the refueling infrastructure challenges that arise because at atmospheric pressure [the pressure at any given point in the earth's atmosphere] DME is a gas that must be stored in mildly pressurized canisters such as those required for LPG [liquified petroleum gas].

Crude oil price at which wholesale prices are equal for DME and diesel fuel ranges from $27 to $36 per barrel. Such surprisingly low DME production costs must be considered together with extra costs of getting DME to the consumer (infrastructure costs) relative to petroleum diesel and potentially lower costs for DME vehicles as a result of lower costs for pollution controls. A preliminary analysis suggests that added infrastructure costs may be roughly offset by the reduced vehicle costs.

China's Fossil Fuel Substitution

So who is leading the way in DME research and production? Why China, of course.

The Hindu [leading English language newspaper in India] is reporting "China to build its largest DME projects"

> China, the world's second largest energy consumer, will start construction of its largest dimethyl ether (DME) project with an annual output of three million tonnes to reduce rising oil consumption.

> Coal-based DME is a clean-burning alternative to liquefied petroleum gas, liquid natural gas, diesel and gasoline.

> Located in Ordos city of north China's energy-rich Inner Mongolia Autonomous Region, the project will cost 21 billion yuan (USD [U.S. dollars] 2.6 billion), the *Shanghai Securities News* reports.

> Compared with the current annual output of 120,000 tons of DME each year, the project will make a huge difference to China's alternative energy sector, the National Development and Reform Commission (NDRC), the top planning body, said.

> Facing oil shortages, China is speeding up efforts to develop oil substitution programmes to reduce its reliance on oil imports and offset the effects of rising oil prices. But as sustained coal supply has remained a challenge for China, NDRC has banned any coal-based DME project with a design capacity lower than one million tonnes.

I had to read that last sentence twice. Logic should dictate that if coal was in short supply one would not be insisting on massively large plants. The real reason is not that coal is in short supply but rather the Chinese economy is at risk of overheating, water supply is a serious issue, and resultant pollution from the plant is a problem.

The bar was set purposely high enough that it would take central bank funding to get projects off the ground and the NDRC could place those projects in areas where the above concerns would be minimized. The end result seems to be a decrease in overall pollution if coal is converted to DME rather than using it straight up.

Clean Coal

The Business Online is reporting "Sinopec to spearhead $2.6bn clean coal project":

> SINOPEC, Asia's largest oil refiner, is leading a clean coal project in China worth 21bn [billion] yuan [benchmark for Chinese currency] ($2.6bn [U.S. dollars], EUR2.1bn [Euros], £1.4bn [British Pounds]).
>
> The Chinese government is trying to develop coal-based fuel on the mainland to reduce its reliance on oil imports and cut key pollutants by 10% between now and 2010.
>
> A potential shortage of natural gas has been worrying both suppliers and customers in China, prompting energy companies to build their own source of fuels.
>
> DME plants cost 10 times more to build than comparable crude refining capacity and one tonne of DME requires three tonnes of water to make, according to Deutsche Bank.
>
> Piped gas distributor XinAo Group is also building a coal-conversion project in Inner Mongolia, which was set to be China's largest before the Sinopec scheme was announced.
>
> XinAo Group's plant, scheduled to start operation in 2009, will have annual capacity for 400,000 tons of DME.

Coal to Petrochemicals

BizChina is reporting "China National Coal Group Corp purchases Harbin coal-to-petrochemicals plant:"

> China National Coal Group Corp is buying a major coal-to-petrochemicals plant in Harbin, Northeast China, where it plans to turn out 600,000 tons of olefin [an unsaturated chemical compound with at least one carbon-to-carbon

double bond, often used to make synthetic textile fiber] products annually using home-grown technology.

The Beijing-based State-owned company, China's second-biggest coal firm, has reached an initial agreement with the Harbin municipal government on the takeover of Harbin Coal Chemical Engineering Co. Ltd.

Within the next three years, China National Coal aims to produce olefin products such as ethylene and propylene, widely used in the production of plastics, said Jing Tian-liang, president of the coal conglomerate.

The plant's annual production target for 2009 also includes 10 million tons of coal and 2 million tons of methanol, compared with the current capacity of 2.6 million tons of coal and 140,000 tons of methanol.

Zhang from the NDRC said that the government was keen to develop alternatives to oil, in order to cushion the Chinese economy from the effect of soaring oil prices.

But companies should also avoid excessive investment in sectors such as coal-to-liquids, Zhang warned.

"Coal-to-petrochemicals is a good way (for China) to cope with high oil prices, but we should develop it with a good awareness of environmental protection and economic returns," said Zhang.

Killer Coal

MonstersAndCritics is reporting "China deal to cut back coal":

The International Finance Corporation [IFC]—the private-sector arm of the World Bank Group—signed a deal with China's Xinao Group to buy shares worth up to $10 million in the company, in addition to providing a $40 million loan for a plant that will convert coal into dimethyl ether. In addition, Xinao will access loans up to $140 million from

Opening China to Energy Efficiency

Efforts to improve energy efficiency are the most effective and affordable measures China can take to meet development goals while reducing greenhouse-gas emissions. Continuing its tradition of relatively impressive energy-efficiency policies, China recently approved new fuel-economy standards for its rapidly growing passenger-vehicle fleet that are more stringent than those in Australia, Canada, and the United States. Moreover, the government has set an extraordinarily ambitious target of cutting energy intensity by one-fifth by 2010.

International partners can help China to build on these important efforts, in particular by promoting the business, financial, and regulatory skills needed for energy-efficiency projects and standards, and to reform policies that impede market-driven projects. Developing incentives for accelerated technology transfer, particularly for the private sector, are also crucial. Many of these efforts are already underway, and Chinese government officials are open to proposals that can help them meet their targets. Foreign partners need to be open and flexible so that their efforts can have maximum impact.

Jeffrey Logan, Joanna Lewis, and Michael B. Cummings.
"For China, the Shift to Climate-Friendly Energy Depends on
International Collaboration," Boston Review, January–February 2007.

commercial banks to build petrochemical facilities that will produce up to 600,000 tons of methanol, the bulk which will be brought in from Inner Mongolia. That methanol will be used to produce about 400,000 tons of DME each year.

Although securing a steady supply of energy is crucial for China to keep its economic engine roaring, the price for explosive growth has often been paid by the country's environment.

Coal is the most readily available and cheapest energy source in China, yet mining for the resource is not only dangerous for miners, but it also causes considerable environmental damage, in addition to releasing toxic fumes when used indoors. Indeed, more than 1 million Chinese die from air pollution each year, with over 60 percent of those deaths occurring as a result of indoor smog, according to the bank.

'This project will help develop new resources to meet China's energy demand and will do so in an environmentally friendly way. Replacing coal with a clean fuel for household cooking and heating has clear health benefits,' said the IFC's executive vice president, Lars Thunell, at a news briefing following the agreement signing with the [World] bank's president, Paul Wolfowitz.

Xinao Chairman Wang Yusuo said that the deal will be as much about profits as it will be about protecting the environment.

'DME is a clean fuel . . . that can replace diesel,' Wang said, and added that the shift toward DME use by public transportation and household use should eventually decrease China's dependency on oil and natural gas, an objective that has been highlighted by the Communist Party [China's ruling government].

'With this project, Xinao is developing a clean energy source that has been identified by the Chinese government as a strategically important alternative to polluting fuel such as coal or diesel,' Wang said. He declined, however, to specify how affordable the DME will be for consumers.

Gauging Successful Transformation

Yet therein lies the key for the success of the project. For while DME may be less damaging to the environment than coal, the ultimate aim will be to ensure that more people are using it over coal, which will depend on a number of factors including its affordability and availability in areas consumers are located.

The [World] bank's director of the oil, gas, and mining department, Rashad Kaldany, pointed out that the agency will gauge how well the project is doing not simply by setting basic numerical targets, but also by monitoring how popular it becomes with consumers, how many jobs it creates, and see how it will affect lifestyles, particularly in energy-intensive cities.

Given that "1 million Chinese die from air pollution each year, with over 60 percent of those deaths occurring as a result of indoor smog[,]" burning coal straight up is not the answer to peak oil. Greenhouse gasses, scarred earth, smog, and respiratory illnesses are some of the problems with coal. Converted into DME, however, many of those problems go away. A reduction in emissions is a start. And China seems serious about reducing those emissions given the size and scope of the projects mentioned above.

China Leads While United States Is Idle

Once again the US seems content to let the rest of the world take a lead. We have up to now concentrated our effort on solving our energy needs on one of the least productive and most expensive ethanol producing alternatives (producing ethanol from corn). We will not even allow the importation of ethanol from Brazil, a country that can produce it at far cheaper prices than we can. Norway, Brazil, Canada, China, and other countries are all developing significant ways to reduce their need for oil and/or are attempting to take advantage on pollution control aspects offered by DME or nuclear power. For now, the US is needlessly bogged down in Iraq and seems content to sit back and watch other countries lead the way.

| *"The costs of cleaning up coal are surprisingly modest."*

Cleaning Up Coal Justifies Its Use

Tim Folger

Tim Folger is a contributing editor to Discover *magazine. In the viewpoint, Folger states that coal is, unavoidably, a key world energy producer. The viewpoint argues for the production of low-cost, coal-based energy with low carbon emissions. According to the viewpoint, the cost to build a new energy grid through a mishmash of options is unrealistic. Retrofitting existing plants and adding advanced technologies to new coal-fired facilities justifies coal's energy future based on cost, ecology, and convenience.*

As you read, consider the following questions:

1. Why is capturing carbon dioxide easier at integrated gasification combined cycle (IGCC) coal plants compared to normal coal-fired plants, according to the viewpoint?

2. What is the biggest obstacle to IGCC plant construction in the United States, according to the viewpoint?

3. According to Folger's interviewees in the viewpoint, how fast could the coal industry adapt to potential mandatory regulations on carbon emissions?

On a steamy, torpid summer morning in Florida, the Polk power plant is performing a small feat of modern alchemy. Every hour it converts 100 tons of the dirtiest fuel on the planet—coal—into 250 million watts of power for about 56,000 homes and businesses around Tampa. The alchemy part? Vernon Shorter, a tall, bluff consultant for the Tampa Electric Company (TECO), points to a looming smokestack. "Look at the top of that stack," he shouts over the cacophony of generators and coal-grinding machines. "That is the main emissions source. You can't see anything. You don't even see a heat plume."

He's right. No smoke mars the lazy blue Florida sky. The Polk plant captures all its fly ash, 98 percent of its sulfur—which causes acid rain—and nearly all its nitrogen oxides, the main component of the brown haze that hangs over many cities. Built to demonstrate the feasibility of a new way to wring economical power from coal without belching assorted toxins into the air, the $600 million plant has been running steadily since 1996. "It makes the lowest-cost electricity on TECO's grid," Shorter says. "It also has very, very low emissions. Particulate matter is almost undetectable."

What is both distressing and remarkable about the Polk plant is that it could do much more. "There's no requirement for mercury capture, but 95 percent of it could be captured very easily," Shorter adds. More important, the plant could also capture nearly all of coal's most elusive and potentially disastrous emissions: carbon dioxide, the main gas that drives global warming.

Soaring Appetite, Soaring Emissions

That capability could prove vital. With oil and natural gas prices rising rapidly and nuclear power stuck in political limbo, the world's appetite for coal is soaring. In the United States, the Department of Energy estimates that 153 new coal-fired power plants will be built by 2025. Meanwhile, China and India, the world's second and third largest coal producers, are embarking on a coal power plant building spree. China alone is expected to construct 562 new coal-fired plants over the next eight years. Since the life span of a typical coal-fired plant is 50 years, coal's share of the world's energy production will rival oil's for most of the century.

Industry advocates brag that the United States, which has 27 percent of all known coal reserves, is "the Saudi Arabia of coal," with enough to burn for the next 180 years at the current rate of use. Unfortunately, coal is as filthy as it is cheap and abundant. When burned it releases three pounds of sulfur dioxide and four pounds of nitrogen oxide for every megawatt-hour [watts measure electrical power as generation or consumption where a coal plant rated for 1000 megawatts (MW) produces 1000 MW at peak operation; a MW is equal to 1000 watts, which is a kilowatt (KW)] of operation. The nation's plants produce a total of about 48 tons of mercury annually. "If all the coal-burning power plants that are scheduled to be built over the next 25 years are built, the lifetime carbon dioxide emissions from those power plants will equal all the emissions from coal burning in all of human history to date," says John Holdren, a professor of environmental policy at Harvard University's Kennedy School of Government.

Holdren and many others are especially concerned about the carbon dioxide, which unlike coal's other emissions is completely unregulated in the United States. By 2012, the new coal plants in the United States, China, and India will send 2.7 billion tons of carbon dioxide into the atmosphere each year. According to leading climate models, all the added CO_2 could trigger an average global temperature rise of up to 10 degrees Fahrenheit [F] by 2100. That much warming could raise sea levels several feet, flooding the world's coastlines and shifting global weather patterns in ways that could cause massive recurring crop failures.

The smoke-free skies above the Polk plant hint at a way out. We now have the technology to capture and store most of the carbon dioxide generated by burning coal. "It's very important what we do with the next 25 years of coal plants," says Holdren. "If all those coal plants are built without carbon control, the amount of carbon dioxide added to the atmosphere would make it virtually impossible to stabilize atmospheric carbon dioxide concentrations at a moderate level." Right now the Polk power plant is one of just four of its kind in the world. If we are going to survive our coal-fueled future, we will probably need a whole lot more like it.

IGCC: Controlled Engineering

The technology behind the Polk plant is called an integrated gasification combined cycle—a mouthful usually shortened to IGCC. Unlike conventional coal-fired generators, IGCC plants don't actually burn the coal itself; they convert it into gas and burn the gas. This highly efficient process makes it possible to selectively pull out the resulting emissions, including carbon dioxide, which could then be collected and buried rather than released into the air.

Vernon Shorter walks through the maze of pipes and towers that is the Polk power plant, giving me a tour of how IGCC works. He points out a conveyor belt that carries a steady stream of coal from a 5,000-ton storage silo to a grinding mill, where the coal is mixed with water. The resulting mudlike slurry is then pumped under 400 pounds per square inch of pressure to the plant's most novel feature, the 300-foot-tall gasification tower.

The tower looks like an unfinished skyscraper, a boxy skeleton of steel. At its top sits a 30-foot-tall vessel filled with 96 percent pure oxygen heated to 2500° F. When the slurry is injected into the chamber, it doesn't ignite. Instead, the coal reacts with the oxygen and immediately starts to break down into its component gases, mostly hydrogen and carbon monoxide. Those gases are cooled and pumped through a series of filters that remove sulfur, particulate matter, and other pollutants; only then is the remaining synthetic gas, or syngas, burned for power.

Shorter then points out the progress of the syngas through a set of pipes descending from the gasifier to a building that houses a combustion turbine—essentially a jet engine mounted on the floor. The syngas ignites inside the turbine, spinning the turbine blades that generate about half the plant's electricity. Torrid exhaust gases from the turbine are captured and used to heat water, which is fed to a separate steam turbine to yield another 125 megawatts. This two-turbine scheme makes an IGCC plant about 15 percent more energy efficient than a conventional coal plant.

IGCC technology also gives engineers unprecedented control over what happens to the different components of coal after they go into the power plant. In normal coal-fired plants, nearly all the pollutants go up the smokestack, where some of them are captured from the exhaust by scrubbers. Here they never even hit the flame. Conventional plants burn pulverized coal in the air, which contains about 78 percent nitrogen. Since the burning takes place at low pressure, the carbon dioxide is diffuse; isolating it is difficult and expensive. Burning gasified coal in pure oxygen at high pressure concentrates the carbon dioxide, making it far easier to capture.

An Energy Future of Bad and Good Investment

Although Polk does not capture carbon dioxide (it still goes up the exhaust stack at a rate of 5,000 tons a day), it could easily be retrofitted to do so; new IGCC plants could have the capacity built in. Shorter reports that TECO is planning to replace this plant with a much larger, 600-megawatt IGCC facility. "The rumor I've heard is that it will be online by 2013. I'm sure the new plant will be CO_2-capture ready. It wouldn't make sense not to. Anyone that's going to build one today has got to be thinking that carbon-emissions permits are going to be required in the future. What do you do when that day comes and you're not ready for it?"

Unfortunately, Tampa Electric's plans aren't typical of the industry. Of 75 coal-fired plants planned for construction over the next decade, only 9 are slated to be IGCC, largely because an IGCC plant costs about $1 billion, 15 to 20 percent more than a conventional one. "The biggest obstacle is simple economics," says Holdren. "There is no incentive for capturing carbon in the United States, India, or China. The most important thing that could happen to drive IGCC forward would be putting a price on CO_2 emissions in the form of a mandatory economy-wide 'cap and trade' approach, which is what a Senate resolution passed last summer recommended."

Although the Senate resolution went nowhere, David Hawkins, the director of the Climate Center at the Natural Resources Defense Council in Washington, D.C., is convinced that the political landscape will change as the effects of global warming become impossible to ignore. Signs of that change are already evident in several states—most notably California, where Governor Arnold Schwarzenegger has introduced legislation that will require a 25 percent reduction in greenhouse gases by 2020. When policies shift, the economics will follow. "We're talking to Wall Street investors and telling them that if someone wants to borrow a billion dollars to build a coal plant and you don't ask them what their strategy is to control carbon dioxide, you're making a very bad investment," Hawkins says.

The Polk plant, on the other hand, has been a very good investment. Tampa Electric actually makes money from the pollutants that the IGCC process removes from the coal. The utility sells sulfur captured from the syngas to the fertilizer industry. Stag left from the coal is sold to the cement industry. All the slurry water is recycled to the gasifier, there is no waste water and very little solid waste. "Almost nothing goes to a landfill," Shorter says.

That squeaky-clean image starts to fall apart, however, as I'm leaving Polk and encounter a dump truck loaded with 54 tons of that black rock. Another truck roils along every 15 minutes or so, 24/7, feeding the plant's 2,400-tons-per-day habit. Some of that coal, no doubt, once lay beneath a mountain in West Virginia. And that chapter of the coal story is anything but tidy. . . .

Carbon Capture: Learn as You Go

Even if IGCC offers no solution to the dangers of pulling coal from the earth, it at least provides a way to control some of the most hazardous by-products of burning (or gasifying) the coal. For some of the captured contaminants, like fly ash, this is a straightforward matter of burying the waste in a landfill. Carbon dioxide is a much trickier proposition. The research on how and where to store it safely essentially forever is just starting.

In September 2005, the Intergovernmental Panel on Climate Change, a United Nations organization that includes scientists from nearly every country in the world, released a report estimating that 2 trillion tons of carbon dioxide could be stored in old coal mines, abandoned oil and gas fields, and in various other geologic formations around the world. That's a huge reservoir, even compared with the rate at which humans are now burning fossil fuels. "The estimated storage capacity equals about 80 times the total rate at which we make carbon dioxide from everything per year," says Robert Socolow, a Princeton University physicist who coheads its Carbon Mitigation Initiative. "Coal-power plants account for about 25 percent of that carbon dioxide, so it's 320 years of coal-power emissions."

Three large-scale carbon storage, or sequestration, projects are testing ways to bury carbon dioxide effectively. The world's oldest carbon-sequestration experiment began in the North Sea oil fields in 1996. Statoil, the Norwegian national oil company, extracts carbon dioxide from natural gas and pumps 2,800 tons of it every day 3,000 feet below the North Sea floor, trapping it in sandstone. A 250-foot-thick layer of shale covers the entire sandstone formation, and it seems to be leakproof. Statoil estimates that all the carbon dioxide emissions from every power plant in Europe for the next 600 years could be stored in the formation.

EnCana Petroleum of Calgary, Alberta [Canada] is conducting North America's first big sequestration project. The company buys carbon dioxide from an American utility and pumps the gas underground in southern Saskatchewan to force out oil that would otherwise be unrecoverable. During the six years that the project has been running, there have been no signs that any of the gas is escaping. EnCana ultimately expects to store about 20 million tons of carbon dioxide underground. A third project, in Salah, Algeria, expects to store 1.2 million tons of carbon dioxide per year in natural gas wells.

"We're going to get more ideas on where to put this stuff," says Socolow. "In a few decades, I think we'll have a sense of the formations we can access, and the numbers will go up. Conceivably, we may find that we were optimistic, and the numbers will go down. But we've got to get going and learn the subject. It's like prospecting; you'll get some unsuccessful ones and some good ones. It's 'learn as you go'—but we're ready to start." All the storage capacity in the world won't matter, however, if we don't have the kind of power plants that can siphon off the carbon dioxide (and other pollutants)

From Coal to Oil

A South African Company, Sasol, has become the world leader in converting coal to oil.

One method for creating a synthetic alternative to crude oil:

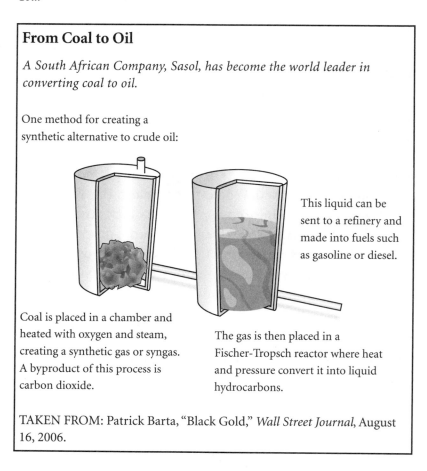

This liquid can be sent to a refinery and made into fuels such as gasoline or diesel.

Coal is placed in a chamber and heated with oxygen and steam, creating a synthetic gas or syngas. A byproduct of this process is carbon dioxide.

The gas is then placed in a Fischer-Tropsch reactor where heat and pressure convert it into liquid hydrocarbons.

TAKEN FROM: Patrick Barta, "Black Gold," *Wall Street Journal*, August 16, 2006.

---

so it can be buried. Nine new IGCC plants over the coming decade will make only a minuscule dent in the problem.

The Energy Future Will Not Wait

Most in the coal industry argue that market forces will sort out the problem, a dubious view shared by the [President George W.] Bush administration, but that seems improbable unless IGCC technology gets cheaper or the cost of emitting carbon goes up. The Department of Energy is aiming to kick-start the technology with a project called FutureGen, a $1 billion pilot IGCC plant that will have integrated carbon-capture and storage technology—a true zero-emissions plant. But the department has not yet even chosen FutureGen's construction site, and the plant will probably not be completed before 2012.

Some companies aren't waiting for FutureGen to get off the ground. Vattenfall, a Swedish firm, is backing a technology called oxyfuel combustion, which burns coal in a nitrogen-free atmosphere. By August 2008, the company expects to complete a 30-megawatt plant near Berlin [Germany] that will capture and store carbon dioxide in an aquifer outside Berlin. BP [British Petroleum energy corporation] is planning a hydrogen-fueled 500-megawatt plant 20 miles south of Los Angeles. When completed in 2011, the plant will make hydrogen from petroleum coke, an oil-refining by-product, in the process storing as much as 4 million tons of carbon dioxide a year in California's oil fields. Still, these also amount to just a drop in the bucket of human-generated carbon emissions.

The Progress Is Getting Scared

So what will it take for emission-free coal technology to go mainstream? Holdren thinks the mounting evidence of climate change will spook the world into action. "I believe that right across the industrialized nations there will be mandatory economy-wide approaches in place by no later than 2010, and in the major developing countries by 2015," he says. James Hansen of the Goddard Institute for Space Studies argues that China and India will make this decision out of pure self-interest, since rising sea levels could place large portions of their coastal populations at risk. China has already committed to a 43 percent increase in industrial energy efficiency by 2020.

"Things could change overnight," agrees Daniel Schrag, a Harvard University geochemist who studies both ancient climate and carbon sequestration. "Think of being involved in airport security in August of 2001. You couldn't have gotten a meeting with the Undersecretary of Transportation. And now it's a month later and you're meeting in the Oval Office."

Schrag suggests that the costs of cleaning up coal are surprisingly modest. "Right now we put about 2.5 billion tons of carbon from coal burning into the atmosphere each year. An order-of-magnitude estimate for capture and storage is something like $100 a ton. That 2.5 billion tons is only $250 billion dollars a year—about half a percent of global GDP [gross domestic product]. It's a lot of money—it requires political will—but it's not a ridiculous amount of money."

For context, Schrag compares that cost to other ways we willingly pay for security. "Solving the climate problem altogether—completely rebuilding our energy infrastructure—is something like a $400-billion-a-year program. The U.S. share is maybe $100 billion. That's not that much compared with defense outlays. It's small compared to Iraq. If we really got scared, we could do a lot in a hurry."

> *"Americans living near coal-fired power plants are exposed to higher radiation doses than those living near nuclear power plants that meet government regulations."*

Coal Cannot Be Made Clean to Justify Its Use

James Finch

In this viewpoint, James Finch points out the environmental bias against nuclear energy that ends up favoring corporate coal mining. Using the Navajo reservation in New Mexico, as an example, he shows how the Navajo Nation has resisted nuclear power and uranium mining in favor of coal. Finch catalogues the dirty secret of those New Mexico coal plant operations: the radiation from coal firing may be more dangerous than uranium-based nuclear power. James Finch contributes to StockInterviews-.com and other publications.

As you read, consider the following questions:

1. According to viewpoint author James Finch, why won't the coal mines of New Mexico be shut down anytime soon?

James Finch, "The Future of ISR Uranium Projects in New Mexico: King Coal and the Navajo," *StockInterview.com*, January 25, 2006. Copyright © 2004–2007 by StockInterview.com. All rights reserved. Reproduced by permission.

2. The Navajo Nation has prohibited uranium mining on its New Mexico reservation, according to the viewpoint. Why haven't the Navajo also prohibited coal mining, according to Finch?

3. According to the viewpoint, environmentalists believe the nuclear power fuel cycle is a potentially dangerous process that can cause harmful public health and environmental problems. Why is there little reporting on the radioactivity released from coal burning, according to the viewpoint?

According to the U.S. Energy Information Administration, about 80 percent of the electricity in New Mexico is generated each year by burning coal. The irony is that the dominant anti-nuclear group in New Mexico, Southwest Research and Information Center (SRIC), has shown no evidence of denouncing coal consumption. According to Don Hancock, an SRIC Administrator who directs the non-profit organization's Nuclear Waste Safety Program, the group's "spiritual mentor" is John W. Gofman. The former nuclear physicist is an aging, eccentric author who was discredited by the Atomic Energy Commission and was branded by the nuclear power industry as "beyond the pale of reasonable communication." As a kind gesture, Hancock gave us a copy of a Gofman "cartoon book," whose theme revolves around [American naturalist and author Henry David] Thoreau's essay, "Civil Disobedience." Another cosmic ally is Amory B. Lovins of the Rocky Mountain Institute, a favorite Don Hancock icon.

While Gofman championed solar energy in his hey day, Lovins presently espouses hydrogen as a primary solution for transportation, wind, and increasing efficiency through natural gas. However, neither wind power nor solar energy is a relevant energy source in New Mexico. Hydroelectricity supplies about 0.7 percent of New Mexico's electricity generation. Despite the hoopla and hyperbole, all of [the] other renewable energy sources combined supply New Mexico with a mere 0.6 percent of its electricity. Coal is, in a very big way, the overwhelming reason why New Mexicans are not living in darkness and without heat or air conditioning.

The Cost of Breathing Coal Production

According to the Harvard School of Public Health, about 2,400 people die every year from the air pollution caused from each million tons of sulfur dioxide emitted. In 1999, it is estimated that over 1.05 billion tons were produced, releasing 11.856 million tons of sulfur oxides and more than 5 million tons of nitrous oxides. Having personally inspected the first floor library of SRIC headquarters, no anti-coal mining literature was discovered. There appears to be scant fund-raising interest from these environmental activists to close down New Mexico's large coal mines. In fact, more U.S. coal mining deaths were reported in 2005 than deaths from uranium mining (zero). *StockInterview.com* heard no worries at SRIC over the blackening of coal miners' lungs, but the staff appeared very concerned over the radon gas [naturally occurring radioactive gas formed from the breakdown of uranium in the environment, and a cause of lung cancer] emitted from uranium mining. Uranium mining in New Mexico came to a standstill about twenty years ago. Coal mining continues as it has for seven decades.

Don't expect the coal mines of New Mexico to be closed any time soon, though. No matter how deadly coal mines are, coal production is irreplaceable at this time. According to the New Mexico Bureau of Geology and Mineral Resources, tax revenues from coal in 2001 exceeded $30 million. Nearly one-half of the state's energy needs are met through coal-generated power. The coal industry employed 1,800 people in 2001. New Mexico is the country's leader for methane gas production from coal beds. Coal is the state's third largest source of revenues.

Navajo Double Standards on Coal

An EPA [Environmental Protection Agency] Toxic Release Inventory report published in 2000 reported that two power plants and their coal mines in New Mexico's San Juan County released 13 million pounds of chemical toxins into the Four Corner's area (New Mexico, Arizona, Utah and Colorado). It was also reported that 6.5 million tons of solid waste was buried by the two San Juan County power plants on their sites or at nearby coal mines. Those airborne toxins were miniscule compared to over 300 million pounds of *other* emissions, such as particulates and nitrogen dioxide released into the air, and which can travel for hundreds of miles. Reports confirm those power plants were among the worst polluters in the United States. The eighth worst emitter was Giant Refining, about 17 miles from Gallup, New Mexico, which emitted 608,000 pounds according to the EPA report. Any visitor to the Gallup area can readily smell the stench circulating in the air.

Why haven't the Navajo banned coal mining on the reservation as they have uranium mining? According to Anna Frazier, a Navajo affiliated with a local environmental group, "Our Navajo Nation is certainly not going to do that. They would rather have the revenues coming in from the coal companies and the power plants." According to a news report published in *Indian Country* newspaper, "The Navajo Nation receives the bulk of its annual $100 million operating expenses from royalties, leases and taxes from its coal, oil and gas. These revenues provide operational expenses for the tribal government, including the salaries of the 88-member Navajo Nation Council, the tribe's annual budgets show."

For more than 35 years, Peabody Energy has operated massive mines on Navajo territory. The closure of one such coal mine, the Black Mesa, sent the Navajos rushing for their Maalox. Ironically, it was environmental activists that forced Southern California Edison to close their Mojave Generating Station nearly 300 miles away in Laughlin, Nevada. The utility

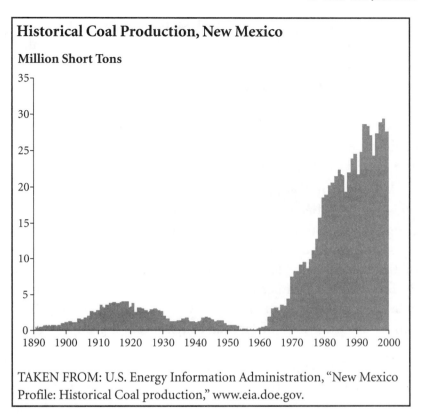

Historical Coal Production, New Mexico

Million Short Tons

TAKEN FROM: U.S. Energy Information Administration, "New Mexico Profile: Historical Coal production," www.eia.doe.gov.

was given a choice: cough up $1 billion to stop polluting the Grand Canyon or shut it down. It had been called "one of the dirtiest coal plants in the West," and air emissions from that plant reportedly polluted half a dozen other national parks in the Southwest. But that coal mine provided about 15 percent of the Navajo's annual budget. George Hardeen, the Navajo president's media voice, complained about the mine closing last October, "This is going to have a terrible effect on this entire region because the Navajo economy is so fragile."

Environmentalist Backlash: Lost Jobs

[Staff writer] John Dougherty complained about the Navajo Nation's tactics in the *Phoenix New Times* newspaper in March 2005, observing, "Environmental groups have long exploited the Native American tradition of sacred places to fight their battles to preserve wilderness areas. . . . It's always the soulful Native American who steps forward as the high priest of sacred geography. In the background lurks the environmentalist equipped with charts and data on tree-trunk diameters and spotted-owl nesting sites." Dougherty concluded, "The cries of environmental destruction and cultural murder from Navajo and Hopi leaders ring hollow."

What are not going to be ringing at all will be the cash registers at Albertsons supermarket in Bullhead City, near Laughlin (Nevada), which closed down this week. That's because the Mojave power station closed as advertised because of the dirty Black Mesa coal. Mike Conner, president of the Bullhead Area Chamber of Commerce, said, "The community will be devastated." Across the river in Laughlin, Buddy Borden of the University of Nevada at Reno told a group of community leaders the area "will take an almost $21 million hit" in lost power plant payrolls. The facility will lay off 375 employees, who had an average annual wage of $87,000. Like dominoes falling, jobs in Nevada, Arizona and in the Navajo Nation were lost.

Recently [as of January 2006], Navajo president Joe Shirley Jr. considered replacing budget shortfalls with casinos, four in Arizona and two in New Mexico. Last March [2005], [Arizona] Senator John McCain forecast the Navajo casinos would fail because of their remote locations. Shirley quipped back in the *Arizona Republic* newspaper, "I beg to differ with him." One coal mine that won't be on the Navajo reservation is the first to receive an operating permit in six years. Peabody Energy announced a coal mine on Lee Ranch, one of New Mexico's largest landowners. It is projected to produce 102 million tons of coal over the next thirty years. For the time being, the Navajos hope to solve their economic quagmire by just putting up more casinos across a New Mexico landscape, already replete with "truck stop casinos." One can soon get bored guessing when the next casino will surface while driving across either Interstate 40 or I-25, the state's main arteries. First you see a sign announcing which tribal land you are entering, then the ubiquitous billboard describing which has-been musical act is "now appearing," and then finally the combination truck stop, casino, restaurant(s) and discount smoke shop whizzes by. One aging Navajo told *StockInterview-.com*, "It's bad for the families, and it sets a bad example for the younger ones."

On Navajo reservation land and just in New Mexico alone, Joe Shirley Jr. may control more than 75 million pounds of uranium, with a gross value presently exceeding $2.7 billion. Some say the number could run much higher, into the hundreds of millions of pounds. Don't expect Mr. Shirley to over turn his ban on uranium any time soon. Dr. Fred Begay, a Navajo and nuclear physicist at Los Alamos, whose career has been featured on *BBC Television* and in the pages of *National Geographic* and celebrated by the New York Academy of Science, explained the problem, "The Navajo don't get it. They think that they'll have miners. They have illiteracy on mining and uranium." Dr. Begay clarified that the Navajo have failed to differentiate between conventional uranium mining and ISR operations [In Situ Recovery mining for uranium, where wells are drilled into the ore zone, circulating the naturally occurring water, and adding oxygen to it, allowing the uranium to become soluble and extracted], which he considers safe, "They think that miners are going in there and digging it out."

The Uranium in Coal: Hypocrisy Reigns

Perhaps the illiteracy about mining extends to geochemistry. Coal is big money in New Mexico, and a little-known fact about the composition of coal may enlighten more than just environmentalists. Former Oak Ridge National Laboratory researchers J. P. McBride, R. E. Moore, J. P. Witherspoon, and R.

E. Blanco reported in *Science* magazine (Dec 8, 1978: "Radiological Impact of Airborne Effluents of Coal and Nuclear Plants") the shocking conclusion that "Americans living near coal-fired power plants are exposed to higher radiation doses than those living near nuclear power plants that meet government regulations."

In an article entitled *Coal Combustion: Nuclear Resource or Danger*, researcher Alex Gabbard, explained, "Coal is one of the most impure of fuels. Its impurities range from trace quantities of many metals, including uranium and thorium, to much larger quantities of aluminum and iron to still larger quantities of impurities such as sulfur. Products of coal combustion include the oxides of carbon, nitrogen, and sulfur; carcinogenic and mutagenic [cancer and mutation causing] substances; and recoverable minerals of commercial value, including nuclear fuels naturally occurring in coal."

Did you know that the amount of radioactive thorium contained in coal is about 2.5 times greater than the amount in uranium? For a large number of coal samples, according to Environmental Protection Agency figures released in 1984, average values of uranium and thorium content have been determined to be 1.3 ppm [parts per million] and 3.2 ppm, respectively. Uranium and thorium are *in* coal. For the year 1982, assuming coal contains those same uranium and thorium concentrations, each typical plant released 5.2 tons of uranium (containing 74 pounds of uranium-235) and 12.8 tons of thorium that year. Total U.S. releases in 1982 (from 154 typical plants) amounted to 801 tons of uranium (containing 11,371 pounds of uranium-235) and 1,971 tons of thorium. These figures account for only 74% of releases from combustion of coal from all sources. Releases in 1982 from worldwide combustion of 2,800 million tons of coal totaled 3,640 tons of uranium (containing 51,700 pounds of uranium-235) and 8,960 tons of thorium. Coal consumption has jumped dramatically since 1982—by more than double!

Gabbard calculated the net impact of the release of uranium and thorium from coal burning by the year 2040:

> Based on the predicted combustion of 2,516 million tons of coal in the United States and 12,580 million tons worldwide during the year 2040, cumulative releases for the 100 years of coal combustion following 1937 are predicted to be:
>
> U.S. release (from combustion of 111,716 million tons):
>
> - Uranium: 145,230 tons (containing 1,031 tons of uranium-235)
>
> - Thorium: 357,491 tons
>
> Worldwide release (from combustion of 637,409 million tons):
>
> - Uranium: 828,632 tons (containing 5883 tons of uranium-235)
>
> - Thorium: 2,039,709 tons

Coal's Daily Tragedies

The population effective dose equivalent from coal plants is *100 times* that from nuclear plants. According to the National Council on Radiation Protection and Measurements (NCRP), the average radioactivity per short ton [2,000 pounds] of coal is 17,100 millicuries/4,000,000 tons [the curie is a unit of radioactivity; the millicurie equals one thousandth of a curie], or 0.00427 millicuries/ton. This figure can be used to calculate the average expected radioactivity release from coal combustion. For 1982 the total release of radioactivity from 154 typical coal plants in the United States was, therefore, 2,630,230 millicuries.

Gabbard explained further: "Thus, by combining U.S. coal combustion from 1937 (440 million tons) through 1987 (661 million tons) with an estimated total in the year 2040 (2516 million tons), the total expected U.S. radioactivity release to the environment by 2040 can be determined. That total comes from the expected combustion of 111,716 million tons of coal with the release of 477,027,320 millicuries in the United States. *Global releases of radioactivity from the predicted combustion of 637,409 million tons of coal would be 2,721,736,430 millicuries."*

Uranium and the entire nuclear fuel cycle are blamed for a host of ills by the anti-nuclear crowd, but little is reported on the subject of radioactivity released from burning coal. Gabbard writes, *"Large quantities of uranium and thorium and other radioactive species in coal ash are not being treated as radioactive waste.* These products emit low-level radiation, but because of regulatory differences, coal-fired power plants are allowed to release quantities of radioactive material that would provoke enormous public outcry if such amounts were released from nuclear facilities. Nuclear waste products from coal combustion are allowed to be dispersed throughout the biosphere in an unregulated manner. Collected nuclear wastes that accumulate on electric utility sites are not protected from weathering, thus exposing people to increasing quantities of radioactive isotopes through air and water movement and the food chain."

While environmental groups hold fund raisers to stop uranium mining, protest the nuclear fuel cycle, and lobby to have vested interest groups, such as the Navajo Nation, ban uranium mining on the reservation, little data or statistics can be found about the daily tragedies found through coal production. There is no vocal outcry from Southwest Research and Information Center about coal mining, let alone the radioactive dangers found in releasing toxic coal fumes into the atmosphere. It was a difficult task to locate the data illustrating, as Mr. Gabbard has done, that the radioactivity *in* coal, from thorium and uranium, is far more deadly than the world's fleet of nuclear reactors. Will Joe Shirley, Jr. now ban coal mining on the Navajo reservation lands? After all, a greater amount of radioactivity is released among the Navajo from coal consumption than uranium mining ever would have achieved. Or will Mr. Shirley let that slide because his budget committee wouldn't stand for it?

"*Coal, then, could well be a major contributor to a transformed energy transportation sector that eventually eliminates its one-third share of greenhouse gas emissions as we build a growing, thriving hydrogen economy.*"

International Partnerships Justify Clean Coal Use

Spencer Abraham

Spencer Abraham was the U.S. energy secretary in the George W. Bush administration from 2001 to 2005. In his speech, Abraham promotes coal as one of the world's great resources, not only as an energy resource but also as a bridge to technological advancements in hydrogen transportation and nuclear fusion. The justification for coal use, according to Abraham, is its durability and longevity as economic and technical drivers to global twenty-first century energy advancements.

As you read, consider the following questions:

1. Abraham states his belief that energy security is a goal that all nations share. What are the essential items of these shared energy security goals, according to the viewpoint?

Spencer Abraham, "Clean Coal Power Conference Speech: Abraham Says U.S. Pursuing Clean Coal Projects with Other Countries," *usinfostate.gov*, November 18, 2003.

2. Abraham states the U.S. goal for the model FutureGen project is virtually zero emissions from a coal-fired electricity and hydrogen production plant. What crucial, technological knowledge will the FutureGen project deliver, according to Abraham?

3. What methods are governments, private corporations, and researchers using to join together for a clean-coal energy future, according to the viewpoint?

I know that many of you have traveled a long way to participate in this Conference. The Department of Energy appreciates your interest in the far-reaching potential of clean coal, as well as the knowledge and experience you will be contributing to the Conference's deliberations over the next three days.

The many representatives here from the American coal, power and general energy sectors are proof of the tremendous interest in clean coal here in the United States. The private sector, testing new technologies and ideas in the marketplace, is largely responsible for the remarkable progress we have made in recent decades.

Government can promote, coordinate and help to fund clean coal research and development activities, but it is the commitment and creativity of private companies, and of the scientists and engineers at our national laboratories, universities and private research facilities, that turn laudable goals into hard realities.

I want to join ... in thanking the Center for Energy and Economic Development, the National Mining Association, the Electric Power Research Institute, and the Council of Industrial Boiler Owners for co-sponsoring this Conference with the Department of Energy.

And I bid a special welcome to the representatives of foreign governments and companies joining us today.

It is a particular pleasure to welcome the delegation from the People's Republic of China. That this Conference is being conducted in conjunction with the Second Joint United States/ People's Republic of China Conference on Clean Energy is added proof of the importance of coal to the world's energy future.

Building Energy Security

The United States is today in the process of implementing and enacting President Bush's far-reaching national energy policy [as of 2003]—a policy that will help guarantee our nation's energy security by ensuring supplies of dependable, affordable and environmentally sound energy for the future.

Clearly, energy security is a goal every nation shares, and President [George W.] Bush has pledged that the United States will be a leader in the long-term effort to achieve that goal. The policies needed for energy security may differ somewhat from nation to nation, but the essentials, we believe, are the same:

- First, we all recognize that energy is too precious a commodity to waste. Good policy begins with the most efficient possible use of energy. More than half of the more than 100 recommendations in the president's energy plan address energy efficiency and renewable energy. In fact, we are seeking more funding for energy efficiency and renewable energy programs this year [2003] than Congress appropriated last year or any year during the last 20 years [between 1983 and 2003].

- Second, we require a balanced and diversified portfolio of energy resources, which in the case of the United States includes coal, oil, natural gas, nuclear power and renewable energy sources.

- Third, we recognize the urgent need to conserve and improve the quality of the environment by reducing emissions from energy production and consumption. Environmental performance is integral to any discussion of energy.

- Fourth, we understand that scientific breakthroughs and technological innovations are essential to achieving our energy security goals, improving the use of today's energy resources and paving the way for a transformed energy future.

- And fifth, we are committed to international cooperation to strengthen energy trade relationships, accelerate scientific/technological progress, and spread the benefits of energy and environmental advances to every corner of the world.

Clean Coal and Hydrogen Energy

Clean coal is a crucial element in our overall policy. President [George W.] Bush has committed the United States to a 10-year, $2 billion clean coal research initiative [in 2003]. Earlier this year [2003], we announced eight projects under the clean coal initiative totaling $1.3 billion—over $1 billion of which will come from the private sector. Clean coal is a cornerstone of our current energy portfolio, particularly for power generation, and it will continue to be for the long-term future.

Not only that, we see the potential for an additional and perhaps equally significant contribution from clean coal. We believe coal will become an important source of the hydrogen that will power the fuel cells that will transform the transportation energy sector in decades to come, as well as contribute greatly to on-site industrial, commercial and residential power generation.

Breakthroughs in scientific research and new technological developments are the basis for past and future advances in clean coal, and cooperative international efforts such as this Conference will speed our progress and spread the benefits of our work.

[U.S. Department of Energy] Sandia National Laboratories researchers here are studying the burning characteristics of coal to prepare the way for the coming of a hydrogen economy. . . .

"While some day we may be able to produce hydrogen by breaking up water molecules in association with the high-temperature heat from nuclear power reactors, or through renewable energy technologies, right now the most cost effective way to produce hydrogen is with coal," says Chris Shaddix, principal investigator for clean coal combustion at Sandia's Combustion Research Facility.

Science Daily, *"Experiments Examine Hydrogen-Production Benefits of Clean Coal Burning," May 10, 2006, www.sciencedaily.com.*

The Popularity of Coal

We have gathered here the right participants for a conference on clean coal. Taken together, the countries represented in this room account for most of the world's coal production and consumption.

The United States, China and India alone account for 37 percent of the world's coal reserves and 46 percent of coal consumption today. Our Energy Information Administration forecasts that world coal consumption over the next 24 years will increase by nearly 50 percent, to approximately 7,500 million tons a year—and the US, China and India will account for 58 percent of that total.

The reasons for coal's popularity are obvious:

- It is the world's most abundant energy resource, with reserves enough to last two to three centuries.

- It is widely dispersed around the world.

- It is among the most economic of energy resources.

- It has been a key source of energy for the world's people since the dawn of history, and

- It has been used extensively, it is being used extensively, and it will continue to be used extensively long into the future.

Black Coal and Clear Skies

Coal is an energy winner with one glaring drawback: it is among the most environmentally problematic of all energy resources. We are here this week to continue the vital work of making coal into one of the cleanest of energy resources, and a valued contributor to a transformed energy future.

We have already made great progress, and we will go much farther in years to come. The more the development and application of new technologies achieves, the more opportunities we see for even greater accomplishments.

In the 30-year period between 1970 and 2000, for example, the United States reduced emission rates of sulfur dioxide from coal-based power generation by over 75 percent, and cut emission rates of nitrous oxides nearly in half. Under President Bush's Clear Skies Initiative [proposed federal law introduce in 2003, amending the Clean Air Act; neither the initiative or its follow up, the Clear Skies Act, made it out of Congress] emissions rates for these two pollutants will drop another 70 percent by the year 2018, just 15 years from now.

Mercury emissions from power generation, which were not considered in previous years, will be controlled for the first time under [the] Clear Skies [Initiative].

And greenhouse gas emissions from coal, which have become a source of concern only in recent years, will be significantly reduced and even eliminated in this century if the President's energy policy is vigorously and successfully pursued.

Partnering on Carbon Capture

Most of the parties in this room are participants in, or share our hopes for, the success of the Carbon Sequestration Leadership Forum [CSLF], a joint initiative of the U.S. Department of State and the Department of Energy. In June of this year, 14 countries, including China and India, as well as the European Union, joined the United States in signing the CSLF's charter. The signatories seek to realize the promise of carbon capture and storage, making it commercially viable and environmentally safe.

Carbon sequestration has rapidly grown in importance to become one of this administration's highest clean coal priorities. Our activities and our plans bear out the determination with which we are pursuing the promise of carbon sequestration.

Current activities include 65 carbon sequestration projects across the country, funded with $110 million in public and private funds.

We have increased this year's budget request for research into carbon sequestration by 50 percent, from the $40 million enacted in last year's budget to $62 million. We are confident that the energy bill now being debated in Congress will ratify our increased funding request.

And, in our most comprehensive action yet, the Department of Energy in September [2003] selected seven Regional Carbon Sequestration Partnerships. The partnerships comprise nearly 150 organizations—among them are federal and state governments, universities and private industry—that span the United States and parts of Canada. The decentralized approach we have chosen will encourage flexibility and creativity, allowing the partnerships to evaluate and promote technologies that are best suited to each unique region.

The Hope of FutureGen

Perhaps our most exciting carbon sequestration initiative is the FutureGen project. FutureGen, as many of you know, is a

$1 billion public-private partnership to design, build, and operate a virtually emissions-free, coal-fired, electricity and hydrogen production plant.

Based on the knowledge and experience accumulated over FutureGen's 10-to-15-year lifespan, we intend to develop and perfect the carbon sequestration technologies that will help make coal-based power and hydrogen production a mainstay of our energy mix. FutureGen has immense potential to change the way we think about coal and its contribution to the world's energy future.

Consider the size of the emissions targets we are aiming at. In the United States, approximately one-third of all carbon dioxide emissions come from power generation, with most of that from coal. Carbon sequestration presents us with the potential, then, to reduce and eventually eliminate nearly one-third of our nation's greenhouse gas emissions.

And that's not all. The transportation sector is responsible for another third of our greenhouse gases. The president's [George W. Bush] hydrogen initiatives are designed to promote the development of hydrogen infrastructure and hydrogen fuel-cell vehicles that could appear on America's roads in large numbers as early as the year 2020. Those vehicles will emit no pollutants or greenhouse gases.

Neither will the FutureGen plants that produce hydrogen to power those fuel-cell vehicles. Coal, then, could well be a major contributor to a transformed energy transportation sector that eventually eliminates its one-third share of greenhouse gas emissions as we build a growing, thriving hydrogen economy.

Coal to Hydrogen

I know that many of you here today plan also to attend the first meeting of the International Partnership for a Hydrogen Economy [IPHE] later in the week. The idea for the IPHE originated with the Department of Energy, and we are pleased with the enthusiastic response generated by the announcement of the first IPHE meeting.

The response proves that many share our enthusiasm for the potential of hydrogen to transform our national economies and make our current preoccupations with energy and environmental challenges into relics of the past.

FutureGen and hydrogen are taking direct aim at as much as two-thirds of the carbon dioxide emitted by the United States. The final one-third of U.S. carbon dioxide emissions is produced by all the other sectors of the American economy. Zero-emissions, hydrogen-producing clean coal will no doubt also contribute to the reduction or elimination of those emissions.

Multiply those long-term advances by similar emissions-reduction achievements in China and India, and the world's other major coal users. Suddenly the long-term challenge of ensuring adequate, dependable, affordable supplies of emissions-free energy begins to seem eminently manageable.

Mobilizing International Coal Efforts

But despite all these interesting programs and possibilities, a significant number of people remain pessimistic about our ability to cope successfully with the energy and environmental challenges we face. President Bush and his administration, emphatically including the Department of Energy and the Department of State, respectfully disagree. As, I suspect, do the people in this room.

Indeed, based on our experience of the amazing scientific and technological advances made in the 20th century, we believe it is difficult not to be optimistic about the world's ability to find timely solutions to these challenges.

Many nations, and many of the world's best minds, have mobilized to create a large network of cooperative, complementary energy research and development initiatives. Governments, private companies, universities, research laboratories and scientists and engineers are joining together to tackle the challenges of clean coal through bi-lateral agreements such as the recent Protocol agreement signed by the United States and the People's Republic of China, and our recent agreement with India to cooperate on clean coal projects.

Multilateral agreements are flourishing. They include the Carbon Sequestration Leadership Forum; the Generation IV initiative for the design of next-generation advanced nuclear power plants; and the ITER project [in Cadarache, France] to harness the power of fusion [the sun and stars produce fusion energy, in which two hydrogen atoms combine to form an atom of helium, during which a partial mass of the hydrogen converts into energy]. They are all clear demonstrations of the determination and commitment of governments around the world to a cooperative approach to future energy security.

The International Partnership for a Hydrogen Economy has the potential to accelerate research and development and eliminate duplication of effort. If successful, it will save money and lead to common solutions applicable in a variety of circumstances.

Pushing to Solve the Energy Equation

We are moving ahead on a broad front, pooling resources, knowledge, experience and capital in an unprecedented, cooperative, international effort to make clean energy the cornerstone of economic growth, improved health and standards of living, and closer ties among nations.

This Conference is a major step toward making clean coal a major contributor to the secure energy future we envision. You are doing your part to turn coal from what many today consider an environmentally challenging energy resource into an essential factor in the solution of the world's clean energy equation.

"In coal mining regions like Mara, the conflict between water and coal boils down to a choice between clean water or regional development."

Local Environmental Costs Do Not Justify Coal Use

Robin Nieto

Robin Nieto argues in this viewpoint that coal mining and production amongst the indigenous populations of Venezuela is not justified. The viewpoint asserts that the cost of coal mining to the ecology of rural peoples' lands far outweighs its potential economic benefit to the overall Venezuela economy. Indigenous Venezuelans, among the poorest population in the country, already face water resource problems; state coal production will only exacerbate their poverty and promote economic ruin. Robin Nieto is a writer for Venezuelanalysis.com.

As you read, consider the following questions:

1. Coal mining contaminates local water supplies in Venezuela, according to the viewpoint. How?

2. According to the viewpoint, coal is a fraction of the Venezuelan economy. Who benefits, then, from mining Venezuelan coal?

3. The government of Venezuelan president Hugo Chavez has told the country that PDVSA, the state oil company, belongs to them. How does this make the job of Venezuelan environmentalists harder?

The government of Venezuela under President Hugo Chávez is supporting a controversial [2004] plan to increase coal mining production in the oil producing state of Zulia. The plan may threaten the state's most important water supply, according to biologists, state water authorities and environmentalists.

Coribell Nava, a biologist and teacher at the Bolivarian University of Venezuela in Maracaibo, says that increased coal mining would mean the destruction of the surrounding environment in the biologically rich Sierra Perija Mountains. The mountains are a vital source of water for Zulia, Venezuela's most westerly state, bordering Colombia.

"Coal is found in the heart of the hydrological valley. The (coal mining) concessions that are being granted in the Sierra Perija would terminate our water source," Nava said.

A Potential Ecological Disaster

Maracaibo, the capital of Zulia, holds over half the state's population of approximately 2.5 million people and depends on only two sources of water in the Perija mountains, the Tulé and Manuelote reservoirs. Both reservoirs are fed by the Cachirí and Socuy rivers respectively.

Corpozulia, the national government's regional development corporation, is planning to open new coal mines along both rivers above both reservoirs. The state water authority, Hidrolago, is also concerned about the national government's plan to increase coal production in the area near the water reservoirs.

"If the coal mining project continues, the ecological impact will be disastrous," Herencia Gonzalez said, the manager of the regional institution of Hidroven, the national government's authority on water.

Gonzalez said that last year she and the Minister of the Environment Dr. Ana Elisa Osorio visited the coal mines currently in operation in the Sierra Perija and said she was shocked by what she saw. "I could not believe my eyes," Gonzalez said, "Is it worth destroying our natural heritage and our water source for coal?" Gonzalez asked.

Indigenous Communities and Coal Mining

The coal mines visited by Gonzalez and Osorio are the Paso Diablo and Norte mining concessions, located just north of the Manuelote water reservoir. Coal mining at these two locations has already displaced indigenous people living in the area. William Fernandez is a 27 year-old student at the Bolivarian University in Maracaibo, and a member of the Wayuu nation. One of 10 brothers and sisters, he and his family were forced to move from their home because of contamination from the coal mines.

"We lived in the Caño Corolado sector by the Guasare River from 1986 to 1995," said Fernandez. "We dedicated ourselves to agriculture, corn, and the raising of cattle. Because of the effects on the environment we had to leave the area."

Fernandez and his family are now living in another region that is also being affected by mining, but this time from Barite mines. "We are now thinking of leaving this area too because of how it affects our animals," Fernandez said.

Families like the Fernandez' are often overlooked by the national government because the population of indigenous communities in the Sierra Perija is small and underrepresented. Communities like the Barí, the Jukpa and the small numbers of Wayuu who have opposed mining have had to do it in the form of protest.

Indigenous territories in the Sierra Perija have yet to be demarcated by the national government and this is something that Rusbel Palmar, a leader within the Zulia indigenous organization, ORPIZ, wants to be settled before new mining projects begin.

"The coal infrastructure plans have not been presented to indigenous people. These plans cannot be done without consultation with indigenous people and different sectors of civil society," Palmar said adding that ORPIZ will not support increased coal production if there are serious environmental consequences. "If the environmental impact assessment finds that there are negative impacts then developments should not continue," Palmar said.

Venezuela's Coal Production Plan

The national government's plan to increase coal production involves hundreds of millions of dollars and includes the construction of a mega port for the international shipping of coal and its extraction by multinational corporations. A thermoelectric plant powered by coal and a railway system to facilitate the transportation of coal from the Sierra Perija mountains to the proposed new port is also in the works. These coal mining projects are set to begin next year [2005] according to Corpozulia.

Corpozulia's plans outlined in the Zulia-wide newspaper, *Panorama*, in an October 27, 2004 article, shows that a large port to be called Puerto America will be built at the mouth of Lake Maracaibo in the Gulf of Venezuela. Corpozulia has predicted investment for this port to total $160 million. The port represents a vital part of the plan to increase coal production.

Further developments include a $946 million proposal to build a 500 megawatt [1 million watts; a typical household lightbulb is between 40 and 120 watts of power] coal-powered thermoelectric plant to satisfy an electricity demand of 2,800 megavolts [1 million volts, where a volt is a unit of electrical potential energy] in Zulia. A railway system for the "clean and efficient" transportation of coal is also in the works with a predicted investment of $281 million.

Scarce Water, a Fragile Ecosystem

In sun scorched Zulia, temperatures run regularly between 30–40 degrees Celsius [86 to 104 degrees Fahrenheit]. The state already faces a chronic water shortage felt not only by the people of Zulia's north-western regions of Mara and Paez, where coal is currently being extracted, but also in Maracaibo where many areas of the city receive running water only once a week.

Recognizing the severe water shortage in Zulia, the national government recently provided a loan of $15 million for water infrastructure for the state's north-western region. However, this water infrastructure would still depend on the two reservoirs currently under threat of contamination by increased coal production.

Coal mining contaminates water through the dumping of waste and coal runoff into the rivers, according to Nava. The biologist explained that coal contains sulphur, and when coal waste and runoff reaches water sources, the water is acidified, making it deadly for those living organisms that depend on the water. This essentially destroys the ecosystem.

Nava also stressed that it is not only the coal itself which affects the rivers that flow into the water reservoirs, but the deforestation that occurs around Zulia's water supply that is part of the coal mining process. "The cutting down of pristine forest is just part of the ecological disaster. The deforestation will also affect the water reservoirs since without trees and their roots to sustain the soil of surrounding mountains, the rain will literally wash the soil directly into the water reservoirs," Nava said.

The health of coal miners will also be directly affected by coal says Nava. "Just as the rivers are acidified with sulphuric acid when coal combines with water, the process also occurs within human lungs leading to an illness called Pneumoconiosis [black lung disease]."

Devil's Choice: Drinking Water or Development?

In coal mining regions like Mara, the conflict between water and coal boils down to a choice between clean water or regional development. For many citizens of Mara who currently depend on potable water from trucks and who receive running water perhaps twice a month, water is more important than both coal and oil.

"We can live without coal and oil but we can't live without water," says 20-year-old Desireé Reverol. Reverol lives in Mara's capital city of San Rafael de El Mojan located along the coast between Lake Maracaibo and the Gulf of Venezuela. This year, El Mojan, as the city is called, was devastated by consecutive days of rain which left unpaved city roads flooded due to a lack of a functioning drainage system.

At City Hall, the new chief administrator, Elio Moran, who came in with a newly elected mayor who supports the national government, says that the most important sources of revenue for the municipality is [a] tax on coal mining and grants from the national government. Moran says that Mara's challenge to develop a public works infrastructure depends on these revenues.

Due to serious infrastructure problems, seasonal rains take their toll on the streets of Mara, where most roads are unpaved and riddled with deep craters and pot holes, the signs of years of neglect. Moran says the region will use the resources provided by both the coal mining industry and development funds by the national government to get the region on its feet.

"Give us 3 months to change things. If after that time things remain the same then we're out," Moran said adding that their number one priority is to get Mara roads in working order, a major overhaul which Moran said will begin in a year, the same time new coal development is expected to begin. Moran also pointed out that Carbozulia, a subsidiary of Corpozulia in charge of coal mining, has offered to donate asphalt towards their road development project.

Poor Water, Poor People

The regions of Mara and Paez, with predominantly indigenous populations, are considered among the poorest in Venezuela.

Due to the lack of a drainage system along roads and a poor sewage infrastructure, rain water mixes with overflowing raw sewage and stays in festering pools all over San Rafael streets for days. And without clean water for such basic necessities such as drinking, washing and cooking widespread illness is a problem each year.

The newly [2004] elected municipal government under 25-year-old Luis Caldera, recognizes the problems their region faces and has pledged to fix them or leave office as Moran has stated. But this promise is based on funding from revenue sources such as coal mining and grants from the national government which depends on oil and increased coal production for its own national revenue.

Mara's development is at the top of Carbozulia's concerns according to Vice-President Enrique Matta who says that the importance of coal mining in Zulia is the revenues it will provide directly to Zulia for development in regions like Mara. "Coal mining will provide resources through a special (national government) development fund for Zulia and in particular to northern Zulia, to the regions of Paez and Mara," Maria said.

Conservation Versus Coal

Environmentalist and biologists say that the cost of coal mining far outweighs the economic benefits that it provides to the state. "Coal today currently represents only 0.02 per cent of revenues for the national government," says Lusbi Portillo, a professor of Logic at the University of Zulia and the head of environmental NGO [nongovernmental organization], Homo et Natura.

"Coal is not very significant in terms of economic production," Portillo said. "However coal is important to other countries like the U.S. which consumes more than 900 million tons of coal each year," Portillo said.

The Ministry of the Environment is in charge of weighing the environmental consequences of development in Venezuela. Back in Caracas, the Vice-Minister of Environmental Conservation, Jose Luis Berroteran, said that coal mining in the Sierra Perija in Zulia is incompatible with the vision of the current national government.

"Coal mining is not in accordance in a country that agrees with the Kyoto Protocol [entered into effect in 2005, the Kyoto Protocol to the United Nations Framework Convention on Climate Change, assigns mandatory limits for greenhouse gas emissions to signatory nations, of which Venezuela is one]. Perhaps coal mining may be acceptable in other countries but not here, not in a country with a government that has a new vision. It runs contrary to policies of sustainable development," Berroteran said.

The conflict between conservation of the environment and coal development is nowhere more obvious than within the national government and its institutions, which are not in agreement when it comes to increasing coal production. While Berroteran does not support further coal development in the Sierra Perija, the Ministry of Environment has yet to ban coal mining along the Socuy and Cachirí rivers that feed the water supply for over a million people in Zulia.

Who Owns Venezuela?

More than 80 per cent of Venezuela's 8.5 million metric tons of coal extracted each year comes from just two mines north of the Manuelote water reservoir, Mina Norte and Mina Paso Diablo.

The coal mines are each owned by mixed companies composed of private and government shareholders. In each case the national government is a minority partner. Carbones de la Guarija operates the coal mine at Mina Norte, 20 kilometers north of the reservoir. The company is a joint venture between the government's Carbozulia and privately owned Carbomar, an international consortium that owns 64 per cent of the mine. Carbomar is composed of the following partners: The Massey Family (30.9 percent); Chevron Corporation (29.94 percent); Meta Corporation (21.56 percent); Art Gommers (8.74 percent); Marcel Van den Berg (8.74 percent); and employees at (0.12 percent).

Carbones del Guasare, which operates the neighboring coal mine at Paso Diablo, 5 kilometers north of Manuelote, is held jointly by Carbozulia, Anglo Coal (24.9%) and new partner, Peabody Energy. Peabody recently purchased 25.5% of holdings from the German mining conglomerate, RAG Coal International, in a deal worth USD [U.S. dollars] $32.5 million. Peabody Energy is the largest coal mining company in the world with annual sales of over 200 million tons of coal and more than $2.8 billion in revenues. According to Peabody's company profile, their products fuel more than 10% of all U.S. electricity generation and more than 2.5% of worldwide electricity generation.

With the strong presence of these and other multinational energy companies such as Tomen America, TransMar Coal and Keysone Coal in the coal mining business in Venezuela, the push to increase coal production in a country with proven coal reserves of over 600 million metric tons may be too appealing for the national government to pass up.

"Coal mining doesn't serve the interests of Venezuelans or Zulians. It serves the interests of coal mining multinationals already operating in the country," says Portillo.

Coal Country's Dark Side

Up a flight of stairs, behind double-enforced bulletproof glass and a large, silent bodyguard sits the office of Francisco Ramirez, a mining-policy researcher and president of Sintraminercol, Colombia's state mineworkers' union. Mining policy really isn't sexy stuff and researching it usually isn't a dangerous occupation, but some of Mr. Ramirez's conclusions can mean life or death, both literally and figuratively. "Once they tried to kill me right here in this office," said the researcher, who has survived seven assassination attempts.

In Colombia's mineral-rich underworld, often demarcated by the full-scale destruction of towns near mining sites, environmental contamination, paramilitary attacks and assassinations against those who stand up to mining interests, Canadian hands are dirtier than those of a coal miner coming up from the pit. . . .

CIDA [Canadian International Development Agency] is supposed to be building schools, providing food aid and doing other touchy-feely "development" in poor countries. So many Canadians will be surprised to learn that the governmental agency, with a $3.74-billion international assistance budget in 2004–05, spearheaded some controversial meddling in Colombia's domestic mining legislation, which, according to Mr. Ramirez, helped "further under-develop Colombia, creating more poverty and decreasing tax revenue for public investment."

Chris Arsenault, "Digging Up Canadian Dirt in Colombia,"
Colombia Journal Online, November 6, 2006,
www.colombiajournal.org.

Like Ploughing the Ocean

Portillo claims that investments for Puerto America will eventually come from the IME [International Monetary Fund and the World Bank are empowered by the group of 7 industrial nations to lend and fund money to impoverished or developing countries] and the World Bank, running contrary to the anti-globalization policies of the Bolivarian government. "Venezuela is serving the (U.S.) empire at our expense and Zulia is a zone of sacrifice," the veteran environmentalist said.

Despite serious environmental concerns about Venezuela's new coal mining plans as well as oil and mineral exploitation, Portillo admits that the environmental movement under the Bolivarian government of President Hugo Chávez is at its weakest point ever, even weaker than during the previous governments. "It's like ploughing the ocean," says Portillo, "In an oil culture where we were taught that oil, coal and minerals make us rich, where can you go?," Portillo asks. "PDVSA (the state oil company) is supposedly ours now, it has been rescued from multinational corporations, this is what people believe, and this makes our work as ecologists even harder," Portillo said.

Protest at the Presidential Palace

Meanwhile Portillo has pledged to protest the coal mining projects at the presidential palace in Caracas in March of 2005. "Five buses will take indigenous people and social organizations from Zulia to Miraflores (the presidential palace) because Chávez should provide compensation for the people affected by coal mining," Portillo said.

The last hope for activists to stop the coal mining plans is direct intervention by the president himself. "Only Chávez can intervene for social reasons," Portillo said.

President Chávez has so far demonstrated support for Puerto America which is vital to increased coal production in Zulia. Many of those against the coal plans support Chávez and the social programs that are part of his Bolivarian platform. However those same people in the communities of the Sierra Perija, in Zulia's universities and even his own environmental authorities, say they cannot afford the environmental cost of the government's enormous coal development projects.

Periodical Bibliography

The following articles have been selected to supplement the diverse views presented in this chapter.

Gary Becker "The Nuclear Option," *Wall Street Journal*, May 12, 2005, www.wsj.com.

Rhett A. Butler "Clean Coal Could Fight Climate Change," *Mongabay.com*, March 13, 2006, www.mongabay.com.

Environmental Integrity Project "Dirty Kilowatts: America's Most Polluting Power Plants," May 2005, www.environmentalintegrity.org.

Jay Hancock "Coal Will Have Role to Play in Nation's Energy Future," *Baltimore Sun*, March 7, 2007, www.baltimoresun.com.

Thomas Homer-Dixon and S. Julio Fried-mann "Coal in a Nice Shade of Green," *New York Times*, March 25, 2005, www.nytimes.com.

Willie D. Jones "Take that Car and Plug It," *IEEE Spectrum*, July 2005, www.spectrum.ieee.org.

Scientific American "Future of 'Clean Coal' Power Tied to (Uncertain) Success of Carbon Capture and Storage," March 14, 2007, www.sciam.com.

Robert Socolow "Can We Bury Global Warming?" *Scientific American*, July 2005, www.sciam.com.

Susan Watts "A Coal-Dependent Future?" *BBC News*, March 9, 2005, www.bbc.co.uk.

Forrest Wilder "The Coal War," *Texas Observer*, November 4, 2005, www.texasobserver.org.

OPPOSING
VIEWPOINTS®
SERIES

CHAPTER 3

Should Coal Use Be Banned?

Chapter Preface

The Apollo Alliance is a combined organization of environmentalists and labor unions seeking to redirect the U.S. economy via employment in, and promotion of, a proposed national clean energy program called the Energy Corps. Apollo believes redirecting the potential U.S. energy sustainability from reliance on foreign oil to cleaner energy production is vital to saving the planet from global warming, would place the United States at the forefront of environmental leadership, and allow unions to regain a stake in the U.S. economy through the creation of green energy jobs.

Van Jones is a civil rights lawyer, a believer in "green-collar" jobs, which 2007 U.S. House Speaker Nancy Pelosi has joined him in advocating, and is an executive director for a human rights organization. In a 2007 interview with *Grist Magazine*, Van Jones stated:

> We need to send hundreds of millions of dollars down to our public high schools, vocational colleges, and community colleges to begin training people in the green-collar work of the future—things like solar-panel installation, retrofitting buildings that are leaking energy, wastewater reclamation, organic food, materials reuse and recycling. All the big ideas for getting us into a lower carbon trajectory involve a lot of people doing a lot of work and that's been missing from the conversations.

The Apollo project controversially supports "clean coal" in the form of carbon capture and sequestration (CCS), collecting carbon emissions from coal plant operations and burying it in deep-mine geology, as part of its clean energy portfolio. Pulitzer Prize winner Ross Gelbspan likes Apollo's environmental mindset but not its coal solutions. He writes:

> Under this strategy, carbon dioxide would be captured from coal-burning power plants and piped into burial areas deep

inside mountains or mine shafts. It is an extremely risky and unproved method of reducing atmospheric CO_2. More to the point, it is extraordinarily wasteful. Even putting aside, for a moment, the question of their efficacy, the cost of a system of carbon sequestration plants amounts to economic lunacy. In this particular proposal, the goals of the Apollo Project and ExxonMobil are virtually identical.

Political commentator Alexander Cockburn argues that global warming is not a major problem, but the politics swirling around it is:

> The sad truth of the matter is that many "big picture" environmental theses such as human-caused global warming afford marvelously inviting ways of avoiding specific and mostly difficult political decisions. You can bellow for "global responsibility" without seriously offending powerful corporate interests, some of which . . . now have a big stake in promoting global warming. The logic of the caused-by-humans models installs the coal industry as the savior of "global warming"? You want to live by a model that does that?

Cockburn does not believe in global warming, yet he does argue that coal plant emissions kill people: "Now, there's no uncertainty about the effects of the stuff that comes out of a power plant chimney. There are heavy metals and fine particles that kill people or make them sick."

One can imagine a scenario in which a variety of organizations that do not agree on global warming might still advocate a ban on coal production and use, replacing it with conservation and green-based, clean energies such as wind, solar, and geothermal. Energy analyst Daniel E. Klein and Duke Business School professor Ralph L. Keeney argue in a 2002 paper that banning, or significantly reducing, low-cost coal fueled-power would, in itself, kill people:

> If coal use were curtailed . . . higher fuel costs would result in higher costs for electricity, which would lead to less dis-

posable income available for U.S. residents to meet other household needs. Numerous studies have indicated that reduction in disposable income results in higher health and safety risks and increased deaths. . . . Simply put, are the potential benefits of the proposed action in terms of expected lives saved greater than the detrimental consequences of the proposed action in terms of expected lives lost?

Banning coal use, like any action associated with the environment and climate change, is controversial. The authors of the following viewpoints argue whether banning coal is a useful action in global and local economies and ecologies.

> "*Banning bituminous coal nationally would improve air quality in the remaining areas of the country.*"

Banning Coal Promotes Public Health

Noel Dempsey and Dan Wallace

Noel Dempsey is the minister for the Environment and Local Government, of Ireland, and Dan Wallace is the minister of state in the same department. In 1990, Ireland banned the burning of bituminous coal in the city of Dublin, later extending it to other areas. The ban, according to Dempsey, yielded a significant drop in pollution levels and mortality, leading to the Irish government's consideration, as of 2001, of banning the marketing and sale of bituminous coal nationwide. Dempsey argues there are no major economic drawbacks to such a plan. Further, he notes, the plan's health benefits are measurably strong based on existing data.

As you read, consider the following questions:

1. Coal burning releases particulate matter, tiny dust particles, according to the viewpoint. Why was this a health problem in Ireland, according to Dempsey and Wallace?

Noel Dempsey and Dan Wallace, "Health and Environmental Effects of Burning Solid Fuel, Bans on Bituminous Coal 1990–2000, and Economic Impacts of National Coal Ban," *Summary of Advantages and Disadvantages of National Ban on Bituminous Coal and Petcoke*, 2001, pp. 4–5, 6–7, 16–17, www.environ.ie/en/Publications/Environment/Atmosphere/FileDownLoad,949,en.pdf. Copyright © 2007 Department of the Environment, Heritage, and Local Government.

2. Why did the Irish government extend the coal ban to five other urban areas beyond Dublin, according to the viewpoint?

3. Why did the Irish consider it more important to ban coal use in the residential sector than in the industrial sector, according to the viewpoint?

Even at non-excessive levels, air pollution impinges negatively on the quality of life for everyone but especially for vulnerable sectors of the population such as the elderly, children, infants and people with respiratory ailments such as asthmatics.

There is increasing evidence that tiny dust particles have harmful effects on human health, causing premature deaths and reducing quality of life. Particulate matter (PM) differs fundamentally from other air pollutants in that it is a complex mixture rather than a single chemical compound, which is emitted into the air by a wide range of man-made sources (e.g. diesel engines, domestic fires, power plants and construction works) and natural sources (seaspray, dust, sand, etc.). PM_{10} refers to small particles less than 10 microns in diameter (10 millionths of a metre) and $PM_{2.5}$ to even smaller particles less than 2.5 microns in diameter. PM_{10} particles are small enough to penetrate the upper airway and $PM_{2.5}$ can penetrate the lungs.

The Black Smoke

The particles produced by domestic coal burning lie wholly within the PM_{10} range with most within the $PM_{2.5}$ fraction. Neither PM_{10} nor $PM_{2.5}$ are new pollutants and the Dublin [Irish capital] smogs of the 1980s are attributable to a mix of suspended particulates or "black smoke" and SO_2 [sulphur dioxide]. Thus, historic levels of both pollutants in many urban areas are likely to have been higher than today's concentrations given the general decline in coal usage and the effects of bans on the burning of bituminous coal.

A significant constituent of PM is sulphur in the form of sulphate which results from the chemical transformation of sulphur dioxide (SO_2) in the atmosphere. A study in the UK [United Kingdom] found that 20% of the total mass of ambient particles sampled were sulphates and that 30% of the total mass in the fine size range (i.e. less than $PM_{2.5}$) were sulphates.

SO_2 is also harmful to humans. Because of its acidic nature it is an irritant to the sensitive tissue of the mucous membranes of the mouth, nose and lungs, and its main impact is on respiratory function. High levels of SO_2 are harmful to human health especially for people susceptible to respiratory problems, such as asthma, bronchitis and emphysema. SO_2 can, through its impact on respiratory function, also aggravate cardiovascular conditions. In addition, there is increasing evidence that small acidic particles which are secondary products of emissions of sulphur and nitrogen oxides affect lung function.

Acid Damage

Acidification means the effects of the introduction of acidifying substances into the environment by means of atmospheric deposition. The primary air pollutants contributing to acidification are SO_2 (mainly from burning of coal and oil), nitrogen oxides (NO_X; key sources are motor transport and power generation) and ammonia (NH_3; almost exclusively from agriculture) which can be carried for hundreds and even thousands of kilometres before being deposited.

While still in the atmosphere, these pollutants can be transformed into acids to be washed out in rain (i.e. "acid rain") onto vegetation, soil, and water. This acidification has extensive biological effects on both aquatic and terrestrial ecosystems which, especially where they have limited capacity safely to absorb excess added acids, can be greatly changed and impoverished by a reduction in the diversity of plant and animal species. Extensive areas of Europe, including some areas in Ireland, have been seriously damaged by acidification.

Acidification results in increased concentrations of aluminium and other toxic metals in the soils, ground water and surface waters. The biodiversity of lakes and rivers is drastically impoverished in areas affected by surface water acidification. Acidified ground water can cause problems, for instance by corroding pipe-work, but in addition by creating health risks through the increased mobility of harmful metals.

Acid deposition also accelerates the rate of deterioration of building materials as well as objects of artistic and cultural heritage, particularly in urban areas.

Dublin's Coal Ban

Following increasing adverse public health and environmental effects of winter smog in Dublin in the 1980s, regulations were introduced banning the marketing, sale and distribution of bituminous coal and high sulphur fuels in 1990. Smokeless fuels became the only legally available solid fuels in the Dublin urban area. On occasions before the introduction of the ban, smoke levels were as high as 7 times the permitted EU [European Union air pollution] limit. Such levels were reached during particularly cold and still weather.

The Dublin ban was very successful with ambient levels of smoke and SO_2 dropping rapidly. In the four years after 1990/91, the 98-percentile smoke value averaged 77 g/m³ (microgrammes per cubic metre) compared with 256 g/m³ in the four years prior to this (the statutory limit value allows only seven values exceeding 250 g/m³ in a full year; three consecutive values of this magnitude also constitutes a breach of the limits).

This successful approach was repeated in Cork City [southern Ireland] and parts of the adjacent county [County Cork]

Decrease in Dublin Air Pollution After the Coal Ban

Black Smoke Average Seasonal Concentrations ($\mu g/m^3$) [micrograms per cubic meter]

Season	1984–90 (pre-ban)	1990–1996 (post-ban)	Change
Autumn	62.4	18.3	−44.1
Winter	85.4	21.5	−63.8
Spring	39.6	10.9	−28.7
Summer	14.4	8.2	−6.2
Total	50.2	14.6	−35.6

TAKEN FROM: Gwyn Jones, Steve Pye and Paul Watkins, "Service Contract for 'Ex-post' Evaluation of Short-term and Local Measures in the CAFE Context," January 22, 2005, AEA Technology. www.airquality.co.uk.

in 1995, when exceedances of air quality limit values were threatened. The ban ensured pollution levels dropped significantly.

Extending the Ban

To meet the [Irish] Government commitment in "*An Action Programme for the Millennium*" to "extend the ban on bituminous coal to major urban areas", five more urban areas (Arklow, Drogheda, Dundalk, Limerick and Wexford) were included in the ban from 1 October 1998. This was further extended from 1 October 2000 to Celbridge, Galway, Leixlip, Naas and Waterford. These bans were based on an analysis of air quality monitoring results over recent years. While mandatory national and EU [European Union] air quality standards were not being breached, these areas had the highest smoke figures nationally and it was recognised that the quality of urban air should be brought to the same standard as obtained in the areas with the bans.

Air quality data and the need for further action is kept under ongoing annual review. However, as not all urban areas monitor for air pollution, it is possible that some towns with no monitoring may have higher pollution levels than monitored areas.

Bans now operate in all cities and many larger towns (covering [approximately] 40% of national population). While smoke levels have significantly reduced, there is evidence of rises in SO_2 levels in some areas (still within national and EU limits) as higher sulphur petcoke [carbon solid derived from oil refinery coker units, it has a low ash content that burns high heat] products replace coal to some extent.

Banning bituminous coal nationally would improve air quality in the remaining areas of the country even though EU and national air quality standards continue to be met. This would be a continuation of the precautionary approach (to avoid deterioration of air quality and to improve it where possible) adopted by the [Irish] Government in extending the ban on a phased basis so far.

The Coal Ban's Social Cost

The Department of Social, Community & Family Affairs (DSCFA) makes a Supplementary Fuel Allowance payment of £3 [3 pounds, British currency] (EUR3.81 [equivalent to US$6]) per week during the winter heating season (October to April, for 29 weeks) to assist lower income families with the increased cost of smokeless solid fuels. . . . The current cost of the scheme is £10m [10 million pounds] (EUR12.697m) [equivalent to US$20.4 million] per annum and DSCFA estimates an extension of the payment nationally would cost an additional £16m [16 million pounds] (EUR20.316m) [equivalent to US$32.6 million] p.a. [per annum, per year] (not including persons on short-term unemployment assistance, some of whom may also qualify).

Payment would be extended to all qualifying persons if a national ban on bituminous coal and petcoke were applied.

The proposed bans are not seen as being sufficiently distorting to require any increase in the Supplementary Fuel Allowance.

Separating Residential from Industrial Uses

In 1999 industry consumed 278kt [kilotonnes] (38%) of the 732kt national total of all types of coal (bituminous, anthracites, lignite, ovoids and petcoke). The residential sector consumed 454kt (62%). 395kt of bituminous coal [medium-soft coal that burns easily] are consumed annually in Ireland. Of this total 99kt (25%) were consumed by industry and 296kt (75%) by the residential sector.

These data are exclusive of about 2 million tonnes of bituminous coal burnt at the ESB Moneypoint power station.

Most coal and petcoke burned by industry and in power generation is or will be covered (by 2002) by the IPC [Integrated Pollution Control] licensing system operated by the EPA [Irish Environmental Protection Agency]. It is, therefore, unnecessary to impose any separate limitations on industry through the proposed ban on the marketing, sale or distribution of bituminous coal and petcoke in the domestic sector.

Low Inflation and a Strengthened Economy

The requirement to supply only smokeless fuels may impact on the price of solid fuel, and have a small inflationary impact on the Consumer Price Index (CPI). Coal (smoky and smokeless) accounts for only approx. 0.83% of the CPI, and an increase of 12% in solid fuel prices nationally (considered unlikely) would be required to increase the rate of inflation by 0.1 percentage point.

Sales of solid fuel nationally have been steadily declining since 1990. Nevertheless, there are currently some 3,000 persons employed in the solid fuel trade nationally.

The Ministers [authors of this viewpoint and members of the Irish government] are of the view that eliminating any scope for use of illegal quantities of petcoke in blends will guarantee a fair competitive environment for the trade. The bans provide an opportunity for legitimate traders to enjoy better security for the trade and facilitate the safeguarding of jobs in these firms. The marketing, sale and distribution of legal fuels only would allow consumers to make straight heating choices based on environmental quality, price, convenience and efficiency without safety worries.

It is recognised that there is increasing competition to the solid fuel market from convenience fuels (e.g. oil and gas), and a ban would also provide marketing opportunities for these fuels.

| "Reality dictates that Texas is going to
need new coal-fired power plants."

Banning Coal Is Unsound Public Policy

Editors, Fort Worth Star-Telegram

The editorial board of the Fort Worth Star-Telegram *argues in this viewpoint that Texas should pursue numerous energy options, including wind, solar, and nuclear. For the editors, though, the bottom-line is population growth, and the population in Texas is expected to rise nearly 50 percent between 2007 and 2030, requiring huge outputs of power generation. According to the viewpoint, there is nothing that can replace the contribution of coal-fired power plants in the Texas economy. Banning them due to ecological motives is downright foolish, according to the authors.*

As you read, consider the following questions:

1. The authors of the viewpoint worry about Texas's having an unreliable electric power supply system. Why?

Editors, "More Coal Power? Yes," *Fort Worth Star-Telegram*, January 28, 2007. Reproduced by permission.

2. The viewpoint notes that a plan to build more coal-fired plants in Texas could contribute to a failure to meet federal air pollution standards. What is a larger contributor to substandard air quality in Texas, according to the authors?

3. What is one of the major advantages of building cleaner coal plants in Texas, according to the viewpoint?

Energy conservation can't do it all when it comes to meeting Texans' growing demand for electricity. Nor can wind power. And it could take more than a decade to get a new nuclear plant built.

Rising electricity demand could leave Texas facing a power shortage by 2010. No one wants a future of brownouts and blackouts.

Reality dictates that Texas is going to need new coal-fired power plants such as the 11 units that Dallas-based TXU [Corporation] is proposing to build. And the state will need them sooner rather than later to ensure a reliable electricity supply that isn't vulnerable to frequent interruptions.

That's the conclusion reached by the *Star-Telegram* Editorial Board after research and conversations with those both for and against the plants, including TXU executives, elected officials, and environmental and public-interest organizations.

Population Stokes Coal Engines

The reason that Texas and the Dallas-Fort Worth area will need more power generation in both the near and long term can be summed up in two words: population growth.

Texas' population is projected to jump nearly 50 percent during the next 30 years, from 23.5 million to nearly 34.6 million, according to a mid-level growth scenario by the Texas State Data Center. The population of 10 D-FW [Dallas-Fort Worth] area counties is expected to swell slightly more than 50 percent by 2030, rising from 6 million to 9.1 million.

This dramatic growth is expected to escalate demand for electricity. Even with significantly increased energy conservation, more juice will be needed to heat and cool homes and offices, power computers, do the laundry and keep the lights on.

The bottom line? Freezing in the dark is not an option. Nor is frying in the brutal heat of a Texas summer. An unreliable electric power supply also could cause good-paying businesses such as computer chip plants to shy away from locating here.

TXU is proposing to build 11 pulverized-coal plants that would be much cleaner and more efficient than those constructed in the past. The plants would have far lower emissions of three major federally regulated pollutants—sulfur dioxide, nitrogen oxides and mercury—than older facilities.

In addition, TXU has pledged to spend $500 million retrofitting four older coal plants. The net result, after the 11 new plants are completed and the older plants retrofitted, would be a 20 percent overall reduction in emissions of the regulated pollutants, company officials said.

A Larger Ozone Polluter

There is concern that TXU's plan would result in greater amounts of polluting emissions blowing into the D-FW area on hot summer days and contributing to the region's continued failure to meet federal air quality standards for harmful ground-level ozone.

We can't say whether that would happen, but the Metroplex [Dallas-Fort Worth area] should put a greater emphasis on reducing emissions from a much larger contributor to ozone pollution: mobile on-road sources ranging from cars to 18-wheelers and mobile off-road sources such as construction equipment.

TXU is seeking permits from the Texas Commission on Environmental Quality to build the proposed plants. Critics

Coal Is Oil?

The Department of Defense has launched a program to develop so-called coal-to-liquid, or CTL, technologies for use in fighter aircraft. On Capitol Hill and in coal state capitals from Montana to Pennsylvania, new incentives and partnerships are stimulating interest in CTL production facilities, creating what energy analysts see as serious momentum for using more of the nation's most abundant energy source.

With global oil prices rising to a new higher floor, the break-even point for costly CTL facilities—between $30-to-$40 a barrel—is here. The result has been significant interest in the CTL area from both industry players and financial investors.

Kraig R. Naasz, "Liquifaction—Expanding the Market for Coal,"
American Coal, 2006, www.americancoalcouncil.org.

complain that coal is a dirty fossil fuel and that TXU isn't planning to use new integrated gasification combined cycle (IGCC) technology that would greatly reduce emissions of carbon dioxide, the major greenhouse gas believed to contribute to global warming. TXU's 11 plants, as proposed, would discharge 78 million tons a year of carbon dioxide.

At present, CO_2 emissions are unregulated, but Congress is considering putting mandatory controls on them.

Regulating Technology and Legislation

TXU officials say that they don't want to use the IGCC technology because it is largely unproven and not well-suited to the Wyoming coal and Texas lignite [softest, with the highest moisture content, of the four kinds of coal] that would burn in the company's new plants. In addition, the IGCC plants probably would cost substantially more and could take longer to build.

We previously have urged that Congress consider adopting legislation to begin regulating CO_2 emissions. But technology to reduce carbon emissions isn't fully developed. TXU officials have said they would build their coal-fired plants so that they later could be retrofitted to accommodate new technologies to capture and store carbon.

We have expressed concern with [Texas governor] Rick Perry's call for "fast-tracking" the permitting process for the TXU plants. This work should be neither rushed nor needlessly drawn out. The process should be conducted at a pace that will allow all interested parties to have their views fully heard.

Additional coal-fired plants are needed, but we can't say with certainty whether all of TXU's 11 proposed plants will be necessary. Changing, currently unforeseen circumstances might dictate a smaller number.

TXU plans to spend $10 billion constructing the 11 plants, which would benefit from a standardized design and economies of scale realized from building such a substantial number. But building a coal plant takes roughly four years, and costs could rise as a result of heavy nationwide demand for new coal plants, with approximately 150 already on the drawing boards [in 2007].

Diversifying Energy

As a result of Texas' adopting electric deregulation, TXU and its shareholders would assume the risk for unexpectedly high construction costs for the plants, company officials have said. That's a stark contrast to the regulated era, when TXU ratepayers took a hit for billions of dollars in construction cost overruns on the company's Comanche Peak nuclear power plant.

One of the advantages of building the cleaner coal-fired plants is that they would reduce Texas' exceptionally heavy reliance on natural gas-fired power plants. Electricity prices have risen sharply in recent years, primarily as a result of increased natural gas prices. Although gas prices have dropped considerably in the past year, they still are substantially higher than in earlier years.

To further diversify its power generation capabilities, Texas should consider building more nuclear power plants, which basically have no polluting emissions. But Texas must increase its generating capacity in much less time than it would take to build nuclear plants. They therefore are only a longer-term option.

We should make this clear: New coal-fired plants are by no means the only solution to meeting Texas' mounting electric power demand in the near term.

A Clean Coal Solution with More Coal Burning

Alternative energy sources such as wind and solar power should continue to be developed and expanded. Texas is No. 1 in wind power generation capacity, but it still meets only a tiny fraction of the state's electricity needs. On summer afternoons when Texas' power demand peaks, wind turbines might generate little electricity because the air often is still.

Energy conservation also should play an increasingly large role in curbing power demand, and the [Texas] Legislature should take steps to mandate that. For example, the state and electric utilities could develop stronger programs to give rebates to consumers for buying more energy-efficient heating and cooling systems and appliances.

Individuals also can help through voluntary actions such as raising their thermostats another degree or two in the summer or putting new insulation in their attics.

Such measures are important, but can't accomplish all that is needed. That's why cleaner coal-fired plants must be part of the solution.

> "If carbon emissions were taxed, a very large fraction of the U.S. coal industry would be promptly shut down."

A Coal Power Ban
Is a Necessity

William Sweet

William Sweet argues in this viewpoint that the United States must end its reliance on coal-fired power plants. Sweet believes it is the coal industry's political power that has shielded it from hidden costs American consumers absorb. Sweet believes the transformation of the coal and carbon industry into clean energy, such as nuclear power, will result from a combination of government regulation, a carbon tax, and shareholder pressure. William Sweet is a senior news editor at IEEE Spectrum, *published by the International Electrical and Electronic Engineers.*

As you read, consider the following questions:

1. Reducing or ending coal power plant emissions runs into a serious obstacle, according to Sweet. What is it?

2. According to Sweet, what issue has split the alliance of midwestern and southeastern coal-burning utilities?

3. Large, institutional investors have begun to make demands on the coal energy companies they hold shares in, according to Sweet. What is that demand and why are they making it?

The correspondences between the oil-fired transportation and coal-fired power sectors are slightly uncanny, a bit like the similarity in size of the Sun and Moon as seen from Earth—that is to say, essentially coincidental, but helpful as memory aids and analytical devices. As [of 2006], estimated yearly deaths from power plant emissions are at least as great as total yearly deaths from drunk-driving accidents, and possibly as great as total traffic fatalities. Each sector, though quite different in terms of how energy is converted and used, contributes about a third of the nation's total greenhouse gas emissions. And each sector, in principle, could make equal contributions to reducing those emissions, which are putting the future of the planet at risk. But doing something serious about automobile emissions runs up against America's love affair with the car, and particularly the gas-guzzling SUV [sport-utility vehicle]. And doing something serious about coal runs up against the immense political power of the midwestern and southeastern coal-burning utilities, an obstacle traditionally believed to be just as high as or even higher than the automotive lobby—though that view may be mistaken.

Same Industry, Different Power

The coal industry is not in fact the immense political force it was fifty years ago, when the United Mine Workers of America [UMWA] numbered more than a million members and its militant leaders, like John L. Lewis and Phil Murray, could threaten to shut down the U.S. economy if their demands were not met. Today, the UMWA has barely more than 100,000 members, many of them retired. Scarcely 70,000 workers actually mine coal, and a great deal of that is stripped by means of huge machines, operated by a handful of nonunion, highly skilled and highly paid men and women. From this perspective, coal might seem almost a spent political force, the stuff of nostalgic songs sung by aging folk-song performers.

From a different perspective, however, the coal industry still exercises almost the same disproportionate sway over the U.S. polity as in the UMWA's glory days. This is because the big utilities in the Midwest and the Southeast rely on it utterly. They are the nation's (and among the world's) very largest utilities, with names like American Electric Power [AEP] (the mightiest of them all), Southern Company, Duke Power, and First Energy. AEP, First Energy, and Cinergy all are located in Ohio, where, increasingly, the closely divided nation sees its destiny decided every four years [due to close presidential elections in 2000 and 2004].

Some measure of the utilities' influence and power can be taken from the events that led to the great Midwest-Northeast electricity blackout of August 14, 2003. That event darkened states from Michigan to New York, as well as Canada's Ontario, making it the largest single outage in history. Though the failure was rooted in the deregulation and restructuring of the U.S. power system, which began in earnest in the early 1990s, both the underlying and the proximate causes could be traced mainly to the negligence of one Ohio utility, First Energy.

Energy Meltdown and Big Questions

The immediate chain of events leading to the August 2003 blackout began two years earlier, when the Davis Besse nuclear power plant operated by First Energy, near Toledo [Ohio], had to be closed down for detailed inspection and reconstruction when unexpectedly severe corrosion was discovered in the vulnerable cap to the reactor core, which is pierced with control rods and fuel rods. Because the situation was so serious—if the corrosion went too far, the reactor's pressurized vessel might burst, releasing vast quantities of radiation into the environment—the Nuclear Regulatory Commission had to order emergency inspection of sixty-nine similar reactors, at considerable expense and inconvenience. Those reactors were found in due course to be all right, but meanwhile, First Energy's Davis Besse plant stayed shuttered, resulting in a shortage of electricity right in the middle of the narrow corridor that connects the midwestern and northeastern power systems.

Beginning early in the afternoon of August 14, [2003] big transmission lines began to fail in First Energy's operating area, several because the utility had not kept up with tree-trimming, so that as heavily loaded lines heated up, they sagged into brush and shorted out. As one went down, the next would become too loaded, sag still more, and short, and so on. All that, the result of a serious infringement of operating standards and no small matter in its own right, would have remained a local problem if First Energy and the midwestern power regulator had quickly recognized what was going on and had promptly cut service to enough customers to keep the whole system from getting overloaded. But the equipment First Energy needed to monitor and simulate what was going on in its system was out of order, and the situation at a newly established regulator in Indiana was not much better. Six months later, when a U.S.–Canada investigatory team reported on the accident, a list of the ways in which First Energy was seriously unprepared for the events that unfolded on August 14 filled the better part of a page. A second list, of the ways in which the utility had violated standard reliability rules, filled another page. Yet there was no talk of imposing civil or criminal penalties. As if nothing noteworthy had happened, the midwestern and southeastern utilities continued to successfully resist federal legislation that would have made reliability rules mandatory and strengthened the hand of the Federal Energy Regulatory Commission [FERC]. In particular, they forced FERC to back off from imposing a "standard market design" requiring all U.S. utilities to play by the same set of rules.

And so, if you ask yourself why burning coal continues to kill tens of thousands of Americans each year, why it still causes neurological disorders in hundreds or thousands of children, why it continues to ravage environments from the Smokies [mountains in southern Appalachia] to the Tetons [Wyoming mountain chain], and why it produces 40 percent of U.S. greenhouse gas emissions each year and 10 percent of the whole world's emissions—and if you ask why so little is done about all that—you need look no further than the amazing events of August 2003 and the role Ohio famously plays every four years in each presidential election.

Fracturing Big Coal

In recent years, however, the alliance of midwestern and southeastern coal-burning utilities has shown signs of fracturing on global warming. In essence the situation is similar to that in the global oil industry, where companies like BP (British Petroleum) and Shell have broken ranks with the mainstream, taking the position that the energy industry is going to have to find ways of weaning the world from carbon-based fuels. Already in the late 1990s, Ohio's AEP, probably the country's largest utility at that time, began to cautiously favor carbon regulation. More recently, James E. Rogers, CEO of Cinergy— the Cincinnati-based utility that emerged as an industry giant in 2005 after merging with Duke Power—has adopted an aggressive public position similar to that taken by BP's [CEO] Sir John Brown. Both Rogers and Duke CEO Paul Anderson have been saying that global warming is a real and very serious problem, and that energy companies can survive in the long term only by addressing it. With Rogers, Brown, and Anderson, personal conviction and vision are clearly playing an important part, but ultimately they are acting in what they see as their corporations' self-interest.

King Coal Comes Black to Texas

Texas ranks as the worst air polluter in the nation for all major categories of air pollutants except sulfur dioxide, where the state is a respectable fourth, according to the national non-profit, Environmental Defense. These dubious rankings have much to do with Texas' dependence on coal for electricity. Although the majority of Texans' electricity comes from natural gas (51 percent), most of the remainder is derived from coal, a much dirtier fuel. (In 2002, coal-fired power plants were responsible for 98 percent of sulfur emissions in Texas, 53 percent of nitrogen oxides, and 60 percent of carbon dioxide from electricity generation, according to the Department of Energy's Energy Information Administration's figures.) In addition, Texas is the nation's leader in mercury emissions from coal power. With the cost of natural gas spiraling upward and national concerns over "energy security," for some the United States' estimated 250-year coal supply suddenly looks like the answer to energy woes. However, by turning to coal—the fuel de jour [of the day] of the industrial revolution—Texas is poised for even dirtier air.

Forrest Wilder, "The Coal War," the Texas Observer, *November 4, 2005, www.texasobserver.org.*

Assessment of such interests is a complicated matter. One factor . . . is that as the United States had adopted strict regulations limiting emissions of sulfur dioxide, utilities burning western low-sulfur coal have had an advantage over the eastern utilities relying heavily on Appalachian coal [with a higher sulfur content]. But if carbon emissions are regulated as well, the western advantage is partly canceled, because eastern coal burns more efficiently and therefore emits less carbon per unit of electricity generated.

Pulling the Carbon Plug

A larger consideration is that as utilities make expensive upgrades to aging coal plants to meet clean air regulations, they worry that if carbon is to be regulated as well, it might make more sense to just replace the plants rather than improve them. Since electricity generated by natural gas is cheaper than coal-generated electricity under most circumstances, and electricity generated by nuclear power plants or wind farms is only marginally more expensive, studies have indicated that if carbon emissions were taxed, a very large fraction of the U.S. coal industry would be promptly shut down.

Last but not least, large institutional investors tend to buy stock in utilities and have an exceptionally large influence on their management. In recent years, many of those institutional investors have been showing up at annual shareholder meetings and demanding that the managers of coal-dependent utilities prepare formal plans for somehow transitioning away from carbon. For example, when shareholders gathered in Tulsa, Oklahoma, in April 2005 for AEP's annual meeting, an activist group warned that the country's number-one carbon emitter risked relinquishing leadership on carbon to Cinergy and Duke. The preceding year, in July 2004, the attorneys general for eight states, including New York, California, Iowa, and Wisconsin, filed suit against a group of energy organizations for producing 10 percent of U.S. carbon emissions: Cinergy, Southern Company, Xcel Energy, AEP, and the Tennessee Valley Authority.

The coal industry's future is hanging in the balance. It should be determined by conscious decisions taken in the broadest public interest.

> *"The lifestyles that produce greenhouse gases are deeply ingrained in modern economies and societies."*

A Coal Power Ban Is a Fantasy

Robert J. Samuelson

Robert J. Samuelson argues in this viewpoint that global coal use is inevitable and essential. Banning coal through media posturing, as promoted by former vice president Al Gore and Hollywood celebrities, detracts from practical solutions to global warming, according to Samuelson. There are no easy solutions, he writes. Probably the best option is coal plant carbon capture and storage (CCS), but CCS has yet to be proved on a large scale. Robert J. Samuelson is a columnist for the Washington Post.

As you read, consider the following questions:

1. What is the difference between the Hollywood version of global warming and the scientific reality, according to Samuelson?

2. Samuelson states that coal use is essential to the world's future. Why?

Robert J. Samuelson, "Hollywood's Climate Follies," *Washington Post*, March 21, 2007. Copyright © 2007 The Washington Post Company. Reprinted with permission.

3. Why does Samuelson think there are no instant solutions to the problems of global warming and energy demand?

"My fellow Americans, people all over the world, we need to solve, the climate crisis. It's not a political issue. It's a moral issue. We have everything we need to get started, with the possible exception of the will to act. That's a renewable resource. Let's renew it."

Al Gore, accepting an Oscar for "An Inconvenient Truth"

Global warming has gone Hollywood, literally and figuratively. The script is plain. As [former vice-president Al] Gore says, solutions are at hand. We can switch to renewable fuels and embrace energy-saving technologies, once the dark forces of doubt are defeated. It's smart and caring people against the stupid and selfish. Sooner or later, Americans will discover that this Hollywood version of global warming (largely mirrored in the media) is mostly make-believe.

Poverty and a Holding Action

Most of the many reports on global warming have a different plot. Despite variations, these studies reach similar conclusions. Regardless of how serious the threat, the available technologies promise at best a holding action against greenhouse gas emissions. Even massive gains in renewables (solar, wind, biomass) and more efficient vehicles and appliances would merely stabilize annual emissions near present levels by 2050. The reason: Economic growth, especially in poor countries, will sharply increase energy use and emissions.

The latest report came last week from 12 scientists, engineers and social scientists at the Massachusetts Institute of Technology [MIT]. The report, *The Future of Coal*, was mostly ignored by the media. It makes some admittedly optimistic assumptions: "carbon capture and storage" technologies prove commercially feasible; governments around the world adopt a

A Crisis of Global Hot Air

There are two great crises in the world of which the biggest unquestionably is four billion people in poverty. And this topic is an ecocondria [made-up word, combining ecology and hypochondria] of our rich selves, London, New York and Washington. It's about us and about our hypochondria about the world. If you actually have clean water, you have modern energy, you will cope with change whatever it is, hot, wet, cold or dry. I'm a left wing critic of global warming because the agenda is fundamentally wrong and dangerous. And believe you me, neither Republican nor Democrat will do anything about it, because our second crisis is a crisis of hypocrisy ... but I come from Europe which has been lecturing the world on this subject. Let me tell you, the hypocrisy in Europe is absolutely mind blowing, I am embarrassed.

Media Transcripts, Inc., "U.S. Global Warming Is Not a Crisis,"
March 14, 2007, comments of Philip Stott,
www.intelligencesquaredus.org.

sizable charge (a.k.a. tax) on carbon fuel emissions. Still, annual greenhouse gas emissions in 2050 are roughly at today's levels. Without action, they'd be more than twice as high.

Coal Is Essential and Substitution Unlikely

Coal, as the report notes, is essential. It provides about 40 percent of global electricity. It's cheap (about a third of the cost of oil) and abundant. It poses no security threats. Especially in poor countries, coal use is expanding dramatically. The United States has the equivalent of more than 500 coal-fired power plants with a capacity of 500 megawatts [equals 10^6 watts of power] each. China is building two such plants a week. Coal use in poor countries is projected to double by 2030 and would be about twice that of rich countries (mainly the United States, Europe and Japan). Unfortunately, coal also generates almost 40 percent of man-made carbon dioxide (CO_2), a prime greenhouse gas.

Unless we can replace coal or neutralize its CO_2 emissions, curbing greenhouse gases is probably impossible. Substitution seems unlikely, simply because coal use is so massive. Consider a separate study by Wood Mackenzie, a consulting firm. It simulated a fivefold increase in U.S. electricity from renewables by 2026. Despite that, more coal generating capacity would be needed to satisfy growth in demand.

Carbon capture and storage (CCS) is a bright spot: Catch the CO_2 and put it underground. On this, the MIT study is mildly optimistic. The technologies exist, it says. Similarly, geologic formations—depleted oil fields, unusable coal seams—provide adequate storage space, at least in the United States. But two problems loom: First, capture and storage adds to power costs; and second, its practicality remains suspect until it's demonstrated on a large scale.

Ugly Economics

No amount of political will can erase these problems. If we want poorer countries to adopt CCS, then the economics will have to be attractive. Right now, they're not. Capturing CO_2 and transporting it to storage spaces uses energy and requires costlier plants. On the basis of present studies, the MIT report says that the most attractive plants with CCS would produce almost 20 percent less electricity than conventional plants and could cost almost 40 percent more. Pay more, get less—that's not a compelling argument. Moreover, older plants can't easily be retrofitted. Some lack space for additions; for others costs would be prohibitive.

To find cheaper technologies, the MIT study proposes more government research and development. The study's proposal of a stiff charge on carbon fuel—to be increased 4 percent annually—is intended to promote energy efficiency and create a price umbrella to make CCS more economically viable. But there are no instant solutions, and a political dilemma dogs most possibilities. What's most popular and acceptable (say, more solar) may be the least consequential in its effects; and what's most consequential in its effects (a hefty energy tax) may be the least popular and acceptable.

The actual politics of global warming defies Hollywood's stereotypes. It's not saints vs. sinners. The lifestyles that produce greenhouse gases are deeply ingrained in modern economies and societies. Without major changes in technology, the consequences may be unalterable. Those who believe that addressing global warming is a moral imperative face an equivalent moral imperative to be candid about the costs, difficulties and uncertainties.

| *"There should be a moratorium on building any more coal-fired power plants."*

Banning Coal Power Is Beneficial

Amanda Griscom Little

Amanda Griscom Little cites climate scientist James Hansen's declaration banning conventional coal-fired power plants to argue that sixty years, the average lifespan of a coal plant, is too long a commitment to this energy source in view of developing clean and green technologies. The economic impact of taking no action on global warming is worse than aggressively decommissioning old coal industries, Little argues. Amanda Griscom Little writes about the environment and energy technology for Grist Magazine. *Her articles have also appeared in* Rolling Stone *and the* New York Times Magazine.

As you read, consider the following questions:

1. Legislation, such as the Global Warming Pollution Reduction Act, has been proposed in Congress, though the chance of passage into law is slim. What is the benefit of proposing legislation that has little chance of passage, according to the viewpoint?

Amanda Griscom Little, "Let's Call the Coal Thing Off," *Salon.com*, March 12, 2007. This article first appeared in Salon.com, at www.salon.com. An online version remains in the Salon archives. Reprinted with permission.

2. According to Little, there is an emerging relationship between Wall Street investors and environmentalists. Where is that relationship being felt, according to the viewpoint?

3. Why do coal-plant performance standards deserve as much attention from politicians as vehicle fuel-economy standards, according to the viewpoint?

Climate scientists, key members of Congress, enviros and the progressive wing of the business world are plotting a coup d'état. Regime change isn't likely to come soon, but this resistance movement could significantly alter the way the pollution-spewing sovereign wields its power.

The ringleader of this uprising is James Hansen, director of NASA's [National Aeronautics and Space Administration's] Goddard Institute for Space Studies and one of the world's top climate scientists. Last week he threw down the gauntlet: "There should be a moratorium on building any more coal-fired power plants," Hansen told the National Press Club.

Coal supplies nearly half the electricity in the United States and is responsible for more greenhouse-gas emissions than any other electricity source. The Department of Energy reported last month [February 2007] that 159 new coal-fired power plants are scheduled to be built in the United States in the coming decade, intended to generate enough juice for nearly 100 million homes.

Bulldozing Old Coal Plants

"If you build a new coal plant, you're making a 60-year commitment—that's how long these plants are generally in use," explains David Doniger, policy director for the Natural Resources Defense Council [NRDC]'s climate center. "So we really need to avoid building a whole new generation of coal plants that use the old technology."

Industry boosters tout the prospect of so-called clean coal, but right now there is simply no such thing. Zero-carbon coal plants—ones that will gasify coal, filter carbon dioxide from the vapor, then stow the CO_2 underground—are a long way away from commercial application. A handful of coal-gasification plants in development could eventually be retrofitted with carbon-capture and carbon-sequestration capabilities, but for now this pollution-storage technology is years away from even a working pilot phase.

"Until we have that clean-coal power plant, we should not be building them," Hansen told his [Washington] D.C. audience. "It is as clear as a bell."

Then the esteemed scientist raised even more eyebrows by declaring that, come midcentury, any old dinosaur coal plants that still aren't sequestering CO_2 ought to be bulldozed.

Aggressive Legislation

Industry reps are scoffing. "Some of Hansen's suggestions are absolutely ludicrous," says energy lobbyist Frank Maisano. "There are fast-growing, rural areas of the country where coal is the only affordable option. Hansen's recommendations would put these areas at risk—they're a recipe for disaster." Maisano added that the NASA's top dog "may be a great scientist, but when it comes to energy policy, apparently he has a lot to learn."

And yet a growing number of policy makers are thinking along Hansen's lines.

[Senator] John Kerry, D-Mass. [Massachusetts Democrat] is drafting a bill that would "prevent any plant from going forward that uses old [coal-fired] technology," said the senator's spokesperson Vincent Morris. Kerry, who chairs the Senate Subcommittee on Science, Technology, and Innovation, expects to introduce the bill in [2007] . . . after ironing out the details on performance standards for advanced-technology coal plants.

"Industry leaders know they are operating in a climate of uncertainty, and that is a very uncomfortable climate for them," Morris says. "They need a clear path charted in terms of the expectations for advanced coal technology, and that's what Sen. Kerry is working on."

The most aggressive climate change bill in the Senate—the Global Warming Pollution Reduction Act, sponsored by Bernie Sanders, I-Vt. [Independent from Vermont], and Barbara Boxer, D-Calif. [California Democrat]—also includes a provision that would require all coal power plants built after 2012 to emit no more greenhouse gases than a combined-cycle gas turbine [CCGT] electric plant, a type of highly efficient natural-gas plant, by 2016. (A similar clean-as-a-CCGT-plant standard is already in effect in California.) By 2030, the Sanders-Boxer bill would require all power plants to be this clean no matter when they came online.

Sending a Signal to Investors

"What that means, effectively, is that you'd have to start phasing in the carbon-sequestration technology as of 2012," Sanders says. "It would offer a big push to get this new technology ready for prime time."

Sanders shares Hansen's emphatic aversion to present-day coal technology: "These plants are destroying the planet! And on top of that they are spewing all kinds of crap that is causing asthma among our children."

It's hard to imagine a moratorium on conventional coal technology being signed into law anytime soon, and yet these proposals still send an important signal. "They make investment in the more advanced coal technology look better to companies and investors because there's less of a regulatory risk," says Doniger.

Even without congressional action, coal's been having a rough go of it lately.

For months [since the beginning of 2007] concerned citizens and enviros had been protesting plans by giant Texas utility TXU to build 11 old-style coal-fired power plants in

What Can Take the Place of Coal?

The *Clean Energy Future for Australia* study has found that Australia can readily meet its energy needs from a range of commercially proven fuels and technologies. A scenario that cuts emissions by 50% includes:

- The energy generated from the combustion of natural gas can provide 30% (including cogeneration) of our electricity by 2040.

- The energy released from biomass from agriculture and plantation forestry residues can provide 26% (excluding cogeneration) of our electricity by 2040

- The energy of wind captured by turbines can provide 20% of our electricity by 2040

- The energy of flowing water harnessed through hydroelectric facilities can provide 7% of our electricity by 2040 and,

- The energy of the sun captured with photovoltaic and solar thermal systems can provide 5% of our electricity by 2040.

- Energy generated by 15% co-generation plants was largely driven by about 13% gas and 2% biomass.

World Wildlife Federation Australia,
"Clean Energy Future," www.wwf.org.

the state. Then, in late February [2007], a handful of private investors proposed buying out TXU for a record-breaking $45 billion, and struck a truce that headed off a lawsuit by Environmental Defense and other green groups by agreeing to cut the number of new coal plants down to three. More surprising, these private entities, which include Kohlberg Kravis Roberts & Co. and Texas Pacific Group, vowed to support a national cap on greenhouse-gas emissions as well as a mandate that TXU invest $400 million in conservation and energy-efficiency programs over the next five years.

"Greening" New Coal Construction

Last week [March 2007], the North Carolina Public Utilities Commission rejected one of two major coal generators proposed by Duke Energy—which, strangely enough, has been on the front lines of the call for federal climate caps. In exchange for permission to build the one plant, the commission said Duke would have to retire four aging coal units and plow 1 percent of its annual retail revenue—about $50 million—into energy-efficiency programs. Duke is now reassessing its plans.

Some environmentalists are bristling over both the TXU and Duke deals, saying that even one new coal plant is too many, and that, in the case of the TXU arrangement, Environmental Defense and NRDC, which also took part in the negotiations, gave up too much for too little. Still, these concessions show that the utility industry is significantly rethinking its relationship to an increasingly embattled energy source—and taking ever more seriously the counsel of environmentalists.

Last week [March 2007], *CNNMoney.com* characterized the negotiations between enviros and TXU's prospective buyers as "the latest sign of how the green lobby is increasingly shaping the agenda on Wall Street."

Ethics and Economics

Said Sanders, "For a long time, industry argued that if we take aggressive action on climate change, it could have negative economic impact. But now the reality is that if we do *not* take aggressive action, the economic impacts of global warming will far surpass those [that the industry] feared would come as a result of regulations."

Moreover, argues Sanders, innovations like coal gasification and sequestration technology have the potential to "reestablish the United States' leadership position in the global economy." India and China are adding roughly one major coal-fired power plant every week, so, he says, "it would be a huge boon for us, ethically and economically, to be able to meet that kind of demand with coal plants that are clean."

The fight to set tougher fuel-economy standards for cars and trucks has gotten the lion's share of attention in [Washington] D.C. discussions of climate policy, but the quest to establish ambitious coal-plant performance standards deserves as much visibility and vigor—for the sake of the U.S. economy as well as the global climate.

> *"We must ... meet the great challenge of this century: helping half of humanity to escape crushing poverty without ruining the ecosystems that make life on Earth possible in the first place."*

Coal Bans Are Based on Indigenous Benefits

Mark Hertsgaard

In this viewpoint Mark Hertsgaard argues that the World Bank, an international lending and economic assistance organization to underdeveloped nations, is not meeting its mandate of lifting the impoverished into the global economy when it funds coal-based projects in the Third World. He argues that energy efficiency might, instead, bridge the gap between the end of coal use and the advent of renewable energy sources. Mark Hertsgaard writes about the environment for various publications and is the author of Earth Odyssey: Around the World in Search of Our Environmental Future.

Mark Hertsgaard, "World Bank on Horns of Dilemma: Key Decision Looms on Oil, Coal Funding," *San Francisco Chronicle*, June 6, 2004, p. E-1. Reproduced by permission.

As you read, consider the following questions:

1. According to the viewpoint, the Extractive Industries Review Commission recommended that the World Bank ban all coal loans to underdeveloped countries as of 2004. Why did the commission feel this was necessary?

2. Why did the Pentagon (the U.S. Defense Department) declare that climate change, or global warming, was a security threat, according to the viewpoint?

3. Hertsgaard believes that Third World coal and oil projects do not help local poor people. Why?

The World Bank [a group of five international organizations, advising and financing underdeveloped nations to create strong economies and eliminate poverty] faces a momentous choice: whether to heed an official recommendation to stop financing oil and coal projects in developing countries. The bank's decision will not only affect the fate of millions of people around the world and billions of investment dollars. It will help determine whether our civilization reverses perhaps the greatest threat of the 21st century: catastrophic global climate change.

The [2004] decision poses a dilemma for World Bank President James Wolfensohn [replaced by Paul Wolfowitz in 2005], for the recommendation to stop funding oil and coal comes from a high-level advisory commission he himself appointed to show that the bank was open to input from civil society and not simply a servant of big corporations, as some activists charged. But Wolfensohn is under pressure from bank management and key member governments, including the United States, to reject the ban. A draft response by management instead urged $300 million to $500 million a year in new funding for coal and oil projects. A vote by the bank's board of directors is expected [in July 2004].

Quitting Oil and Coal

The recommendation to quit oil and coal came in January [2004] from the Extractive Industries Review Commission. Chaired by Emil Salim, a former environment minister of Indonesia but also a former board member of a coal company, the commission included representatives of industry, unions, developing country governments, indigenous peoples and nongovernmental organizations. Citing the dangers of climate change and the often punishing human rights and pollution effects on local people, the commission urged that the bank halt all coal loans immediately and all oil loans by 2008. It further urged the bank to increase renewable energy loans by 20 percent a year and to grant people the right to veto projects they don't want.

These changes would amount to a virtual revolution in the bank's operations and have an enormous effect on both energy policy and corporate behavior in developing countries. Although the bank provides only a small portion of the financing for a given coal or oil project, its influence is immense, because private corporations see the bank's stamp of approval as a guarantee that their own considerably larger investments will be safe. So if the bank stops funding coal and oil, many projects probably won't go forward.

That's exactly what activists hope.

Between 1992 and 2002, they point out, the World Bank approved more than $24 billion in financing for 229 fossil fuel projects. Over the course of their lifetimes, these projects will generate almost double the amount of carbon dioxide that humanity as a whole produced in 2000.

Global Warming: A Poor Person's Disease

An elite Pentagon planning unit [of the U.S. Defense Department] recently declared that climate change was an urgent national security threat that could cause megadroughts, mass starvation and even nuclear war by 2020. Scientists warn that climate change will punish the world's poor most of all. The

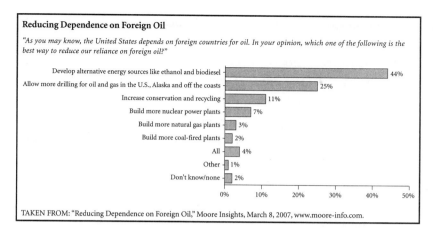

Reducing Dependence on Foreign Oil

"As you may know, the United States depends on foreign countries for oil. In your opinion, which one of the following is the best way to reduce our reliance on foreign oil?"

Develop alternative energy sources like ethanol and biodiesel	44%
Allow more drilling for oil and gas in the U.S., Alaska and off the coasts	25%
Increase conservation and recycling	11%
Build more nuclear power plants	7%
Build more natural gas plants	3%
Build more coal-fired plants	2%
All	4%
Other	1%
Don't know/none	2%

TAKEN FROM: "Reducing Dependence on Foreign Oil," Moore Insights, March 8, 2007, www.moore-info.com.

World Health Organization estimates that 160,000 people a year already die from the effects of climate change. That number will increase as higher temperatures lower crop yields and expand the range of disease-bearing mosquitoes.

But the plight of the poor is also cited by opponents of the proposed oil and coal ban. Like it or not, they say, oil and coal are the cheapest forms of energy available. To rule them out may sound compassionate, but it will actually keep poor countries poor. "We don't like [the proposal] at all," South Africa's minister of minerals and energy', Phumzile Mlambo-Ngcuka, told the *New York Times*. "We think it takes an ideological approach rather than a practical one."

Unfortunately, most Third World oil and coal projects do local poor people little good. A study by the Institute for Policy Studies in Washington found that 81 percent of the World Bank's oil and coal loans went to projects whose output was not consumed at home to build the local economy; rather, that coal and oil was exported to the United States, Japan and other wealthy nations. Thus the poor end up subsidizing the rich.

Spinning in Place

The World Bank should not be contributing to that perverse outcome. Salim, the commission chair, said in an interview with Reuters [news agency] that private capital should remain free to pursue oil and coal projects on its own, but the World Bank's funds should be used to promote renewable energy technologies that the market has not yet embraced. Over the past 10 years, the bank's funding for coal and oil has outpaced that for renewable energy sources by a ratio of 17 to 1. Had the bank instead increased funding of renewables by 20 percent a year, as Salim's commission now urges [in 2004], solar and wind would be much closer to competitiveness [as of this writing].

The bank claims it is changing course. At a meeting in Bonn, Germany, [in 2004] Peter Woicke, [then] the World Bank Group's managing director, promised a 20 percent annual increase in renewable energy funding. By 2010, Woicke said, this increase would double the bank's current pace of $200 million a year in renewable energy lending. But Steve Kretzman of the Institute for Policy Studies called Woicke's announcement "nothing but spin."

"According to the bank's own numbers it has averaged about $420 million a year in renewable energy during the past 14 years. Now Woicke is promising to reach $400 million year by 2010. That's going backwards."

Upgrade Humanity and Life on Earth

In any case, the most urgent short-term focus for the bank is not renewables but energy efficiency. No, it's not sexy. But insulating drafty apartment buildings, replacing old furnaces and motors and installing super-efficient light bulbs is the fastest and cheapest way to "produce" energy in today's world.

Energy efficiency is no silver bullet, but it can be a bridge. It can buy humanity time to get solar, wind, and other green energy sources up and running—as we must, if we are to meet the great challenge of this century: helping half of humanity to escape from crushing poverty without ruining the ecosystems that make life on Earth possible in the first place.

> "Improvement in air quality happened
> during the same time-period that the
> use of coal for generating electricity in
> the United States almost tripled."

Coal Bans Are Based
on Bad Science

Center for Energy & Economic Development

*Environmental special interest groups are trying to guide public
policy decisions by using data and scientific studies that some
experts believe is unsound, according to the Center for Energy &
Economic Development (CEED). CEED describes, in the viewpoint, how environmental advocacy groups misuse scientific
studies to justify their own agenda while ignoring the public
health record of the Clean Air Act. Banning coal power based on
faulty analysis would be misunderstanding this issue, according
to CEED. The Center for Energy & Economic Development is a
nonprofit coal industry advocacy group.*

As you read, consider the following questions:

1. The requirements of the Clean Air Act were phased in
   over time, according to the viewpoint. What benefit did
   this provide the public, according to CEED?

Center for Energy & Economic Development, "Before You Accept Claims That the
Public Is at Risk Due to Exposure to Power Plant Emissions . . . Check the Fine Print!"
www.ceednet.org, February, 2003. Reproduced by permission.

2. What two bodies of research have environmental advocacy groups been using to push their agenda, according to the viewpoint authors?

3. Why are studies based solely on statistical analyses flawed, according to the viewpoint?

Whether in Washington, DC or in state capitals across the country, protecting the public's health and welfare is the number one priority of government policy makers. From past experiences, we know that quality science must be the foundation for developing policies to protect our citizens. Without sound science, the effects of such policies will be uncertain and, in some cases, the unintended consequences can be devastating.

Special interest groups are now trying to shape energy and environmental policies by using science that many qualified experts deem to be questionable at best. These special interest groups allege that the public is at risk due to emissions from coal-based power plants. These groups claim that current emissions standards are not sufficient to protect the public from increased respiratory illnesses or even premature death. But before accepting this claim, there are some key facts that you should consider.

Coal, the Clean Air Act, and Public Health

To put this debate in context, Congress first enacted the Clean Air Act in 1970 to protect the American public from the risks of pollution. This law was amended in 1990 to include a more stringent set of standards. The federal Clean Air Act is one of the most effective environmental laws ever passed, and provides the backdrop for numerous programs that regulate emissions from coal-based power plants. It is the expressed intent of Congress that standards established under the regulatory programs emanating from the Clean Air Act be set at levels low enough to protect human health with an extra margin of safety. The Congress also recognized that overall air quality is the true measure of assessing human health risks. After all, the air we breathe is affected by automobiles, pollen, industrial sources, natural conditions (like wildfires), as well as emissions from power plants.

The regulatory standards established under this law have been carefully phased in to allow sufficient time for the development and deployment of new technologies. This common-sense approach helped keep electricity costs low while dramatic improvements in air quality took place—providing a win-win situation for the American public.

How much has America's air quality improved? Emissions of criteria air pollutants (those defined by the Clean Air Act as having the potential to adversely affect human health) are 25 percent lower today than in 1970. This improvement in air quality happened during the same time-period that the use of coal for generating electricity in the United States almost tripled.

Effective Regulations Require Quality Science

Despite the ongoing success of the Clean Air Act, some environmental advocacy groups suggest that existing clean air laws do not provide adequate protection to the American public. They don't acknowledge the progress being made, and they discount future emissions reductions that will occur under existing clean air laws. These environmental special interest groups say state and federal governments should enact rigorous new regulations for the electric power industry. While their intentions may be good, these groups have used an inherently faulty methodology to produce several studies aimed at shaping the public policy debate. Unfortunately, good intentions without quality science result in bad public policy. Flawed regulations do not provide additional protection to the American public and can often do more harm than good.

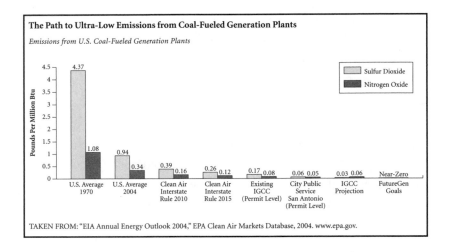

The Path to Ultra-Low Emissions from Coal-Fueled Generation Plants

Emissions from U.S. Coal-Fueled Generation Plants

TAKEN FROM: "EIA Annual Energy Outlook 2004," EPA Clean Air Markets Database, 2004. www.epa.gov.

"Exaggerating the public's risk from air pollution is no better than ignoring real air quality concerns. If society misspends scarce resources based on inaccurate information, more people will suffer, not fewer." —Reason Public Policy Institute, 2002

Flawed Research Is Not Reliable

To make their case, several environmental advocacy groups are primarily using two bodies of research. The Clean Air Task Force (CATF) developed one series of studies, including *Death, Disease and Dirty Power*; and *Power to Kill*; plus several reports that attempt to examine local impacts of pollution. While the titles of these studies were designed to attract media attention and alarm the public, experts have found numerous flaws in the studies' research methodology.

Another study, conducted by [health-care economist] C. Arden Pope and several colleagues, examined the link between exposure to fine particulate matter ($PH_{2.5}$ [particulate matter smaller than 0.0001 of an inch]) and lung disease. Some environmental advocacy groups were quick to misuse the Pope study to advance their policy agenda. According to one group of experts who reviewed the Pope study, "There is nothing in the paper that links, in a medical sense, $PM_{2.5}$ with any diseases and no such causal connection has been made in scientific research."

Because of the concerns raised by experts who have identified flaws in the methodologies used in these studies, these reports should not be considered as reliable tools for policy makers.

Flaws in the Environmentalist Argument

In both cases, the studies were based solely upon statistical analyses, which are no substitute for the clinical studies needed to determine actual risk. Statistical studies often do not adequately control for personal health risk factors such as smoking, alcohol use, and other critical factors. By comparison, clinical laboratory studies of the effects of $PM_{2.5}$ on humans and animals largely find no harmful effect at realistic concentrations. Perhaps more fundamentally, both the CATF and Pope studies assume that all $PM_{2.5}$ is the same. This assumption is not in any way supported by scientific findings. By understanding a little more about $PM_{2.5}$, it is easy to see why this assumption is not valid.

$PM_{2.5}$ is the collective term for thousands of different particles smaller than 2.5 microns in diameter (0.0001 inch). These particles are grouped together and classified as a pollutant merely because of their common size. They can differ in form, surface characteristics, chemical composition, and their ability to dissolve and stay in the lungs. Because of these great variations, different types of $PM_{2.5}$ can have a variety of effects on human health, possibly including no effect at all.

Environmental advocacy groups and others have wrongly assumed that particulate matter from power plants has the same effect on human health as tire particles, vehicle emissions, construction debris, molds, pollen, bacteria, and viruses, including smallpox—all of which are forms of $PH_{2.5}$.

These studies also do not appear to have addressed issues related to indoor air quality. If so, that is another important flaw because, according to current estimates by the American Lung Association, indoor air quality is two, three, five, and, in some cases, even up to 100 times worse than outdoor air.

Narrowing Pollution Controls Harms the Public

The bottom line is, when it comes to protecting the public's health and welfare, we can't necessarily accept things at face value. Policy makers need the best possible analyses to determine whether more stringent regulations to reduce power plant emissions will provide a measurable benefit to the American people. Otherwise, they run the risk of needlessly raising consumer energy prices and focusing pollution control efforts in the wrong direction—which may, ultimately, do more harm than good.

When deciding that existing clean air laws aren't tough enough, make sure you understand both sides of the issue— because it is always best to check the fine print.

Periodical Bibliography

The following articles have been selected to supplement the diverse views presented in this chapter.

The Australian	"Brown Backs Eventual Coal Export Ban," *The Australian*, February 9, 2007, www.theaustralian.com.
Andrew Bartlett	"Time to Get on with Practical Solutions to Climate Change," February 11, 2007, www.andrewbartlett.com.
Sean Captain	"Turning Black Coal Green," *Popular Science*, April 8, 2007, www.popsci.com.
Martin Creamer	"Let's Counter Global Anti-Coal Pressure Jointly, Queensland Premier Urges South Africa," *Mining Weekly*, March 22, 2007, www.miningweekly.co.za.
Friends of the Earth Australia	"Coal Ban Needed," *Friends of the Earth Australia*, February 9, 2007, www.foe.org.au.
Luminus Maximus	"Ban the Bulb?" *American Thinker*, April 3, 2007, www.americanthinker.com.
Faye Mallet	"Black Coal: An Industry in Debate," *Galt Global Review*, February 21, 2007, www.galtglobalreview.com.
Katherine Mieszkowski	"Coal: Clean, Green Power Machine?" *Salon.com*, April 3, 2007, www.salon.com.
Elizabeth Williamson	"The Green Gripe with Obama: Liquefied Coal Is Still . . . Coal," *Washington Post*, January 10, 2007, www.washingtonpost.com.
Kelpie Wilson	"Renewables Can Turn Tide on Global Warming," *TruthOut*, February 2, 2007, www.truthout.org.
Brian Wingfield	"TXU's Seeing Green," *Forbes.com*, March 9, 2007, www.forbes.com.

OPPOSING
VIEWPOINTS®
SERIES

CHAPTER 4

Is Coal Mining Safe?

> *"Here was a separate race of creatures, subterranean, gnomes, pent up by society for purposes of its own."*
>
> —*Upton Sinclair,*
> *from his 1917 novel King Coal*

Chapter Preface

The *International Journal of Injury Control and Safety Promotion* published a 2005 study of injury in Indian coal mines, attempting to understand what are the risk factors for mine work injuries. The two major factors contributing to mining accidents, according to the study, were a negative attitude and job dissatisfaction.

U.S. coal companies sometimes complain they are caught between government regulators, environmentalists, and unions. Regulations overburden miners with safety gear, promote negative attitudes, and swamp employers in compliance paperwork, making it difficult for them all to operate efficiently. In this situation, the coal industry might explain, it is more expensive and stressful to extract coal from the ground, which leads to work injuries and deaths.

Much depends on definitions of legality. Look to a world where regulations are lax or difficult to enforce; look to China. The boom in Chinese coal mining has been due to the world's fastest growing economy, as of 2007, requiring huge volumes of energy, especially electricity, to drive it forward. In this situation illegal coalmines have sprouted across the Chinese rural countryside.

Shanxi province sits by the dried up Fen River, once a tributary to the great Yellow River. State-owned coal companies have ruined the river and destroyed the underground aquifers that helped supply water to what had once been a farming community. Residents of the province have survived by moving from a decimated agricultural economy to illegal coalmining. Local authorities estimate that approximately 500,000 Shanxi province residents are employed in illegal mining operations.

Illegal miners supply cheap coal to residents, for home heating and cooking, to small businesses and even large power and steel companies who cannot meet energy supply needs for their factories. Ma Jun Sheng, a doctor in the Shanxi village of Shi Gou, told the *San Francisco Chronicle:* "There's coal dust everywhere, which causes lots of disease—lung cancer, tuberculosis, asthma. And then there are the accidents. I've been here 16 or 17 years, and there's one every month. The most common problem is collapses. Sometimes the people don't know about the [methane] gases that get released, and so explosions also happen."

Coal mining remains attractive to rural Chinese because it pays two to three times that of farming. Shanxi authorities have no records on coal mining injury and death rates, but China's legal mines have one of the world's worst safety records. Illegal coal mining has also spawned illegal power plants. The *Associated Press* reported in 2006 that rural Inner Mongolia had constructed ten illegal power plants, producing 8.6 gigawatts of electricity, about one-tenth of the United Kingdom's electrical capacity. The illegal plants helped spawn more illegal coal operations.

Li Yizhong was described as China's busiest minister in 2005. The Chinese government placed him in charge of investigating all mining accidents throughout the country. Li Yizhong and a committee of the National People's Congress have both consistently cited corruption, resulting from China's coal rush, as the reason behind nine out of ten Chinese mining accidents.

Robert Chambers, a U.S. federal judge, offered another perspective on illegal mining. He ruled March 23, 2007, that the U.S. Army Corps of Engineers did not have the legal authority to allow mountaintop coal mining methods (using explosives to remove mountaintop layers to get at coal deposits), and the depositing of those waste materials into Appalachian headwater streams, many of which had been buried. Stream destruction has been allowed under the mining policy of the George W. Bush administration purportedly to meet U.S. energy needs but also to increase coal industry profits.

As of 2007, the world has an insatiable appetite for coal. The pressure to produce the necessary harvest falls on engineers, politicians, regulators, and coalminers. How much does the cultural pressure surrounding coalmining affect those involved in it, and how dangerous does that make coalmining? The authors of the following viewpoints offer various arguments as to whether coalmining is safe or not.

> "New machinery such as longwall sys-
> tems have not only reduced the total
> number of workers needed, but done so
> especially at the most dangerous spots."

The Coal Industry Will Make Coal Mining Safer

Edward Rappaport

In this viewpoint, Edward Rappaport argues that health and safety in the coal industry has steadily increased since 1925 because of productivity gains and machinery. Rappaport believes that accidents, such as the 2006 Sago Mine explosion in West Virginia, while tragic, aid the mining industry and Congress in designing safer work environments. Edward Rappaport is an analyst in the Industry Economics, Domestic Social Policy Division of the U.S. Congressional Research Service, a nonpartisan, government agency that provides research analysis on topics of interest to Congress.

As you read, consider the following questions:

1. According to Rappaport, reductions in coal mining fatalities can be attributed to two main factors. What are they?

Edward Rappaport, "Coal Mine Safety," *CRS Report for Congress (Order Code # RS22461), The Library of Congress*, June 23, 2006, www.ncseonline.org/NLE/CRS.

2. How much progress in coal miner safety can be attributed to the Mining Safety and Health Administration, according to the viewpoint author?

3. Congress proposed safety legislation after the Sago Mine accident, according to the viewpoint. What are the four core components of the Mine Improvement and new Emergency Response Act (MINER), according to Rappaport?

On January 2, 2006, the nation was reminded of the dangers of underground mining, as 12 miners died in an explosion and fire in the Sago mine in West Virginia. Subsequently, the Mine Safety and Health Administration (MSHA) issued new regulations; Congress has passed the first major revision of the mine safety law since 1977 and has taken further bills under consideration; and state legislatures in West Virginia, Kentucky, and Illinois have tightened their own laws. These responses have emphasized factors thought to have played a part in the Sago tragedy, including emergency oxygen supplies, tracking and communication systems, and deployment of rescue teams. There have also been proposals to increase the penalties for violations of safety standards. . . .

Safety in the coal industry has undergone a steady trend of improvement since 1925, an era when hundreds of miners could be lost in a single incident. In that year, there were a total of 2,518 fatalities in accidents, whereas the number has since fallen almost continually, down to 22 in 2005. Some of this trend is explained by a decrease in coal industry employment (from 749,000 in 1925 to 110,000 currently) and other structural changes in the industry, but much of it by real safety improvement. Thus, the overall annual fatality rate decreased over the period from 3.36 per thousand workers to 0.20 per thousand. Nevertheless, mining of coal and other minerals remains one of the most dangerous sectors in which to work, with its fatality rate being more than seven times the average for all private industry, and exceeding that of many industries generally thought to be dangerous, such as construction and trucking. In terms of more ordinary accidents (non-fatal), mining is not far from the all-industry average, and indeed there is less variation overall among these industry groups. In what follows, the concentration is on fatal accidents.

Safety Increases Without MSHA

Statistically, most of the 7.6% per year reduction in fatalities per ton (the average rate of improvement over the period 1980 to 2004) can be attributed to productivity (i.e., fewer workers on the job), most of the rest coming from a reduction in fatalities per actual worker. Some is also attributable to an ongoing shift from underground to surface mining. In truth, what lies behind all these factors is mechanization. New machinery such as longwall systems have not only reduced the total number of workers needed, but done so especially at the most dangerous spots (e.g., the active cutting face). Other measures, which have prevented many large-scale accidents, include controlling coal dust, monitoring methane gas (which is both explosive and poisonous), adequately supporting roofs, and avoiding spark-producing equipment.

It would be very difficult to determine conclusively how much of the progress in safety has been due to MSHA. Although the most important safety measures are found in MSHA standards, it could be argued that many mines would have adopted them without that inducement. And indeed, safety had been increasing for a long time before MSHA's founding. Be that as it may, all parties involved agree that there is still room for improvement, but they disagree on the specific course to be followed. The United Mine Workers union has often contended that MSHA has not been sufficiently active. It contends that there are not enough inspectors and that penalties, both as proposed and as negotiated, are not large enough. In general, the union would make enforcement of standards the highest priority. The mining industry generally supports MSHA's existing regulatory approach, although it has urged that inspections be focused on mines where problems are evident, rather than regularly spread among all mines as currently required.

Areas for Improvement

Some recent, widely publicized incidents have highlighted specific areas that may merit further attention. The flooding of the Quecreek Mine in Pennsylvania in July 2002 raised questions about the accuracy of underground mine maps and their availability to operators of nearby mines. The Quecreek accident might have been avoided if the mine operator had access to the final map of a nearby abandoned mine that had since filled with water. In response, $10 million was appropriated to MSHA (in Labor Department appropriations for FY [fiscal year] 2003) for collection and digitization of abandoned mine maps and new technologies for detecting underground voids. In response to the Jim Walter No. 5 mine accident in Alabama in September 2001 (which took 13 lives), MSHA made a number of changes, including a new standard on mine emergency response. The mine workers union alleges that MSHA had not followed up properly on numerous previous violations at the site.

The Sago explosion, caused by lightning that penetrated underground and set off a methane explosion, killed only one miner initially. Sixteen miners escaped; 12 survived the explosion but were trapped and succumbed ultimately to carbon monoxide from the ensuing fire. The episode raised a number of issues. It has been suggested that communication and tracking devices currently available might have enabled the trapped miners to escape or find better refuge, or rescuers to reach them more quickly. Emergency breathing apparatus issued to the miners were rated for only one hour, and reportedly a number of them did not work well. Also, there has been criti-

Less Dangerous than Thought

Mining is safer than most realize. Kentucky's coal industry has a slightly lower injury and illnesss rate (8.21 per 100 workers) than the state's average rate for all workers (8.24) for the 1996–2002 period.

Bill K. Caylor, "Mining Is Safer than Most Realize,"
Louisville (KY) Courier-Journal, *February 2006,*
www.courier-journal.com

cism of the fact that it took 11 hours from the explosion until rescuers entered the mine. (Ironically, though, one of the "lessons learned" from the Jim Walter case may have compounded the problems at Sago. Because most of the victims in the former incident were responding to a relatively small explosion when a larger one occurred, considerable time was taken at Sago to verify the state of the mine atmosphere before rescue crews were sent in.)

Improved Dust Control Decreases Lung Disease

Accidental injuries can be quantified much more reliably than the extent of occupationally caused disease. It is clear, though, that coal mining is causing disability much more by way of long-latency disease than by traumatic injury. Prime among these diseases is black lung (coal workers' pneumoconiosis [CWP]), which still claims about 1,000 fatalities per year (down by about half since 1990). The deaths tend to occur after a long progression, so that only about one year of life expectancy is lost on average for these cases. However, this is usually preceded by many years of impaired breathing and debilitating weakness, as well as many more cases not counted as fatalities (ending with death by other causes). As of 2002 (the latest year tabulated), there were 16,000 cases on the rolls of the black lung program (i.e., deemed totally disabled).

Improved dust control requirements have led to a decrease in prevalence of the disease since the 1970s. Among miners with 20–24 years of work experience, for example, the proportion of examined miners who had positive x-rays decreased from 23.2% in the mid-1970s to 2.2% in the late 1990s. While this is a great improvement, there is still dispute about whether the current dust limits should be lowered, as well as questions about the degree of compliance by mine operators with current limits.

An Emphasis on Emergency Response

The Mine Safety and Health Administration (MSHA) is charged with overseeing the safety of coal and other mining industries. MSHA's budget of $278 million (FY 2006) is somewhat less than the $472 million of its sister agency, the Occupational Safety and Health Administration (OSHA), but OSHA is responsible for protecting a far larger number of workers. MSHA oversees a mining industry (including surface operations and all other minerals besides coal) of about 200,000 workers, whereas OSHA is responsible for most of the rest of the economy. Thus, while OSHA must target its inspections mostly on firms with the worst accident records in a few sectors (notably manufacturing and construction), MSHA is able to cover its whole industry. Indeed, it is mandated to inspect each underground mine at least four times a year and each surface mine twice. In addition to financial penalties, and in contrast to OSHA, MSHA has direct authority to immediately shut down dangerous operations.

Substantively, the regulations promulgated by MSHA cover a wide range of equipment, procedures, certifications and training, including methane monitoring, dust control, ventilation, noise, electrical equipment, diesel engines, explosives, fire protection, roof support, hoists and haulage, maps, communications, and emergencies.

In the wake of the Sago accident, the agency was criticized by many for its slow pace of rulemaking in recent years, allegedly dropping 18 proposed standards that had been pending as of January 2001. The Administration has said that it was pursuing a revised agenda and that it was being more frank by no longer listing long-term projects that had not been making much progress. Since the outset of 2006, however, MSHA has started action on a number of measures. As mentioned, the recent emphasis has been on emergency preparedness and response. A new temporary standard (with formal rulemaking for a permanent standard) was issued on the subject of evacuations, which includes provisions for additional breathing apparatus (self-contained self-rescuers—SCSRs), additional training on SCSRs, escape guides ("lifelines"), and prompt notice of emergencies. Requests for information and proposals were issued for communications and tracking technologies, rescue chambers and rescue teams. MSHA indicated it will revise its penalty assessment formula and has asked the Congress for an increase in the authorized maximum from $60,000 to $250,000.

New Sampling Technology Is Promising

On the matter of preventing black lung and silicosis, MSHA is expressly required by its authorizing statute to enforce a dust control standard. The limit is currently [as of 2006] set by regulation at 2 milligrams/cubic meter as an eight-hour average "for each miner in the active workings of each mine," although NIOSH [National Institute of Occupational Safety and Health] has recommended a limit of 1 mg.

Besides the limit itself, there has been continual controversy about how concentrations are to be measured in the mines and how MSHA will monitor operators' plans and performance. In July 2000, MSHA proposed new regulations (superceded by revised proposals in March 2003) under which its inspectors would verify plans and performance by directly collecting single full-shift samples, rather than the previous practice of multiple samples retrieved by the operators. This proceeding was suspended on June 24, 2003, in favor of the development of personal dust monitors (PDMs), a new technology that could give personalized, real-time readings of dust concentration and finesse longstanding disputes about how air samples are to be handled. Initial tests of PDMs have been promising.

Congress Refines the Safety Process

Much legislative activity, at both state and federal levels, has occurred in response to the Sago and other accidents in early 2006. The most prominent measure has been the Mine Improvement and New Emergency Response. Act (MINER), ... which went from introduction to passage in about three weeks [in 2006]. Among the major points in this bill:

- *Emergency Preparedness.* Each mine to have a plan which includes coordination with local emergency agencies, tracking and communication devices, and a two hour oxygen supply with each miner plus supplementary supplies positioned along escape-ways.

- *Rescue teams.* Each large mine to have two teams familiar with the mine (including a "knowledge-able" mine employee), available within one hour. More flexible rules for smaller mines (fewer than 36 employees). Limitations on legal liabilities of teams.

- *Penalties.* Willful violations may be subject to imprisonment and fines up to $250,000 ($500,000 second offense), compared to current $25,000 ($50,000). Up to $220,000 civil penalty for "flagrant" failure to correct cited conditions. MSHA empowered to seek court orders to collect penalties.

- *Sealing of abandoned mine areas.* MSHA to issue new standard, with strength criterion greater than current 20 pounds per square inch pressure resistance.

Further Safety Standards

While S. [Senate bill] 2803 had broad bipartisan support (passed by unanimous consent in the Senate and under suspension of the rules in the House [allowing noncontroversial legislation to be passed quickly by limiting debate and prohibiting amendments]), some Members characterized it as only a "first step," to be followed by more measures. For example, as compared with S. 2803, H.R. [House of Representatives bill] 5389, [and] S. 2798 . . . would feature:

- additional specific safety measures, including continuous monitoring of the mine atmosphere, refuges stocked with five days of supplies (these measures to be enforced by a withdrawal order if found to be lacking), and a lower limit on dust concentrations;

- more stringent requirements for rescue teams, e.g. that they must be composed exclusively (in larger mines) of mine employees and be immediately available for deployment;

- public hearings and family involvement in accident investigations, which are to be conducted independently of MSHA if so requested by miners' union or majority of affected family members;

- stricter penalties, e.g. $1 million penalty and entire-mine withdrawal order if "pattern of violations" identified; fines to be paid into escrow pending appeals; elimination of consideration of mine size or financial viability;

- a safety ombudsman within the Department of Labor Office of Inspector General; and

- implicitly, a shift of budgetary resources from technical support to enforcement personnel.

> "The Democrats, like their Republican counterparts, subordinate the safety of coal miners to the profit needs of the coal industry."

The Coal Industry Will Not Make Coal Mining Safer

Samuel Davidson

Samuel Davidson argues in this viewpoint that the administrations of presidents Bill Clinton and George W. Bush failed to enact legislation, procedures, and safety regulations that would have saved miners' lives. These failures, coupled with deregulation of the coal industry, have created the conditions that make coal mining a deadly occupation. Samuel Davidson is a writer for the Socialist Equality Party, U.S.A.

As you read, consider the following questions:

1. Does the United States utilize the same safety equipment widely found in foreign countries, according to the viewpoint?

2. The U.S. Mining Safety and Health Administration (MSHA) has said that underground refuge stations are a new technique that potentially could save miners' lives during a mine emergency. How new is the idea, according to the viewpoint?

3. Mining conveyor belts can be used for two different purposes, according to the viewpoint? What are they and how do they relate to mine safety?

Most if not all of the deaths this year [2006] in US coal mines could have been prevented if safety measures proposed for nearly two decades had not been blocked and eventually killed by officials from the [President Bill] Clinton and [President George W.] Bush administrations.

In recent years [up to 2006] officials from the federal Mine Safety and Health Administration (MSHA), under orders from the Bush White House to promote a "partnership" with the coal companies, have overturned several safety procedures in place for years and drastically reduced the enforcement of existing safety standards. In addition, government officials have not mandated the use of safety equipment widely used in other countries that has proved to save lives and prevent injuries.

A Failure to Regulate Deadly Conditions

To date [2006] 21 coal miners have died on the job this year in the US. Another three miners working in metal and non-metal mines have also been killed. The most recent fatalities occurred on February 16 and 17 [2006]. On the first date, 33-year-old Tim Caudill was crushed to death when a section of roof fell at the TECO coal mine near Hazard, Kentucky. On the following day, 35-year-old William Junior Miller was crushed to death between two coal cars in an underground pit in Maryland.

While the investigations into this year's [2006] fatal mining accidents—including the Sago Mine [West Virginia] disaster that killed 12 West Virginia miners—are still continuing, initial evidence indicates that the elimination of previously existing federal and state regulations, the suppression of additional regulations and the lack of enforcement of existing regulations all played a direct role in these tragedies.

Thirteen of the 21 fatalities in 2006 have been the result of asphyxiation after an initial fire or explosion. While it appears that one of the miners was killed instantly by the January 2 blast at the Sago Mine, it is possible that several of the other men trapped underground may have lived at least 10 hours after the initial explosion, according to notes recovered from one of them. The only survivor, Randall McCloy, Jr., was rescued after 42 hours underground but suffered severe brain damage.

Another two West Virginia miners, killed in a January 19 conveyor belt fire at the Aracoma Alma Mine, were overcome by smoke.

Suppose They Had Better Respirators

Each of the 13 miners who died from asphyxiation was equipped with a respirator that provided only one hour's worth of oxygen. On September 24, 2001, MSHA withdrew a proposal that required mine owners to stock caches of additional respirators that would give miners more time to escape or be rescued.

Another portion of the rule change quashed by MSHA would have required more training on the use of the respirators known as Self-Contained Self-Rescuers or SCSRs. These devices are more complicated than the type of oxygen masks found in airplanes. Since pressurized oxygen containers would be an explosive hazard, SCSRs produce oxygen through a chemical reaction. Working them requires miners to perform several steps to start the chemical reaction that supplies a clean airflow.

The Safe Haven Concept

The founding principles of any emergency escape plan in an underground coal mine must be to seek to evacuate the mine with minimum complication and delay. However, for a number of reasons this may not be possible and alternative survival strategies based on the use of safe havens (refuge stations/bays) and self rescuers are required. The use of refuge stations or safe havens can enhance the viability of self-rescuers [apparatuses that provides oxygen] either by providing a location to change a person-worn short duration self-contained self-rescuer for a longer duration unit or alternatively by providing a separate sealed life support system. As [a 1997] report concludes, potentially, the safe haven concept, if developed effectively, has a vital role in establishing a robust emergency survival strategy for use in large hot mines or where there are significant gradients impeding passage out of the mine.

DJF Consulting LTD, "Refuge Stations/Bays and Safe Havens in Underground Coal Mining," Report prepared for the Underground Coal Mining Safety Research Collaboration (UCMSRC), May 2004.

There have been repeated incidents in which the failure to properly train miners in the use of these devices and to have sufficient supplies of the respirators had fatal consequences. In 1987, a MSHA report on the death of 27 miners in a Utah mine three years earlier found that the miners had not been properly trained in the use of the device and that there were not enough of them in places accessible to the miners.

George W. Bush's appointee to head MSHA, David Lauriski, could not complain of being ignorant of these findings when he withdrew the proposal to mandate mine operators to provide more SCSRs. In 1984, Lauriski was the safety and training director at the Utah mine where the 27 miners were killed.

Waiting for Rule Changes

Though the Bush administration killed the proposal for the SCSRs, the Clinton administration had simply delayed its implementation when it was in charge of MSHA until it lost office. The Democrats, like their Republican counterparts, subordinate the safety of coal miners to the profit needs of the coal industry.

It is noteworthy that the head of the MSHA under Clinton, Davitt McAteer, who helped stall the implementation of the respirator proposal, is now in charge of the Sago Mine investigation in West Virginia.

It is useful to take note of the timeline on the enactment (or non-enactment) of mine safety improvements. The terrible mine accident in Utah, killing 27 miners, occurred in 1984, under the [President Ronald] Reagan administration. In 1987, under the Reagan administration, MSHA issued its reports and proposed that ventilation standards be revamped. The Clinton administration, which came into office in 1993, began studying changes to mine ventilation standards. In 1999, after seven years of study—virtually the entire time Clinton was in office—MSHA announced it was ready to "begin the process" of making rule changes. The proposals were then left for the next administration to enact—a measure that virtually guaranteed they would be killed. The Bush administration, elected with the support of Big Coal, did precisely that, withdrawing the proposals in 2001.

While consideration of proposals that would save workers' lives are dragged out for years or decades, Congress has no problem expediting the passage of laws that benefit the wealthiest layers of the population. When it comes to tax cuts for the wealthiest 1 percent of the population, for example, there are no proposals for years of analysis on the effects of such giveaways on the economy, the federal deficit or the ability of the government to maintain social programs.

Rescue Chambers

Another three proposals that in all likelihood would have saved the lives of the miners in both the Sago and Alma [West Virginia] mines were blocked in a similar fashion. The use of refuge stations or rescue chambers has received some attention in the press. In January [2006], 72 potash [chemical in wood used to make glass, soap, and fertilizer] miners in Saskatchewan in western Canada survived nearly 30 hours after a fire broke out in their mine. Earlier that month, three nickel miners in Tasmania [island that is part of the Australian state] survived a fire because they found refuge in an underground chamber equipped with adequate supplies of oxygen, food and water.

MSHA officials and much of the media have suggested that refuge stations are a new and novel idea and that the United States simply needs to catch up with technological changes introduced in other countries. In fact, a report in the *Charleston Gazette* revealed that in 1969—37 years ago—Congress wrote mine and safety laws, following the 1968 Farmington [West Virginia] mine disaster [an explosion that killed 78 miners], that authorized federal officials to mandate safety chambers pending the outcome of a study.

The study, completed in 1970, found that such chambers would be beneficial and specifically refuted objections—still being made today by coal companies and their allies in government—that safety chambers could not withstand explosions or work underground. For 36 years, officials from MSHA and its predecessor knew about these findings, sat on them and never mandated their use in coal mining, despite having the explicit authority to do so.

Refusing to Mandate Lifesavers

The other two proposals that never saw the light of day involved employing advances in communications equipment to allow rescuers to communicate with and locate trapped miners. Since at least 1992, federal mine safety officials have refused to mandate the use of life lines—a rope made of fireproof material attached to the wall of a mine tunnel—that would direct miners safely even out of a smoke-filled mine if lighting had been destroyed by a fire or explosion.

Evidence indicates that the 11 miners who survived the initial explosion in the Sago mine at first tried to escape and then returned back to the coal face—in the deepest part of the mine—in order to build a barricade to preserve fresh air and await rescue. Why they did not continue toward the mine exit is still an open question, but they may have believed there was a cave-in or a fire blocking their route. Under those conditions, the miners did as they had been trained to do.

If the trapped miners had had a means of communicating with rescuers on the surface they could have told them their exact location, allowing rescue teams to reach them sooner. The miners might also have been told that there was no fire blocking their exit and that it was safe to walk out of the mine while using their respirators.

Like the rescue chambers and other safety equipment, MSHA officials claim the communication devices are still unproven. Again, this is not true. There is adequate data proving the effectiveness and reliability of such communication devices, including their role in several mining disasters over the last 10 years [1996–2006], some of them in the US, where they were credited with saving miners' lives.

Fire in the Hole

Finally, there are two additional issues that relate directly to the January 19 [2006] conveyor belt fire at the Aracoma's Alma Mine [owned by Massey Energy, West Virginia] that led to the deaths of two miners. In 2001, Bush administration officials killed a proposal to test the advantages of having conveyor belts made with fire-resistant materials. Like the SCSR proposal, this came out of the Clinton administration, which studied the issue for seven years and then passed it onto the Bush government. A 1992 MSHA report noted that belt fires were shown to be the cause of 14 percent of underground mine fires between 1970 and 1990.

The second issue concerns the use of conveyor belt tunnels as both a means of carrying coal out of the mine and as a pathway to bring fresh air in. Safety experts and US law since 1969 have opposed this practice on two principal grounds: First, pushing high velocity air through a beltway can spread the flames of a belt fire and push toxic fumes directly to the face of the mine where most of the miners are working. The second objection of safety experts is that this dual usage eliminates an alternate path of escape for the miners in the event of a fire, explosion or roof cave-in.

For these reasons, the use of beltways as fresh-air intakes was restricted by MSHA, which mandated that they would only allow the double utilization of such pathways if individual mines applied for and were granted a waiver. Such an application was made by the Alma mine and approved under the Clinton administration in 2000.

For [six] years, coal operators lobbied for MSHA to abolish the restriction altogether. Coal operators were eager to save the cost of digging the separate ventilation shaft, and they felt that the process of applying for permission on a case-by-case base was too cumbersome. In 2003, then-MSHA director Dave Lauriski proposed re-writing the standards on ventilation to allow mines to use the belt entry as a fresh air intake. The new rules were implemented in 2004.

> *"The automated system will improve mine safety by removing people from hazardous environments underground, and it should open up lower-grade deposits and those that are difficult to mine."*

Technology Will Make Coal Mining Safer

Tim Thwaites

The public and media have mostly viewed the mining industry as inherently dangerous. According to viewpoint author Tim Thwaites, the mining operations of the near future will introduce automated machinery to ore extraction and remove humans to safe distances from the coal mine itself. Not only will this lead to greater productivity, according to the viewpoint, it will enhance health and safety for the entire industry. Tim Thwaites is a writer for earthmatters.

As you read, consider the following questions:

1. According to the viewpoint, who are the only personnel who will enter automated mines?

2. The Remote Ore Extraction System (ROES) described in the viewpoint integrates new technologies. What are those technologies, and how do they reduce mining costs, according to the viewpoint?

3. Who drives the vehicles that remove coal at the Olympic Dam mine in South Australia, according to the viewpoint, and how do the vehicles increase mining safety?

The first thing that strikes you is the relative lack of people wearing the conventional miner's gear of the 20th century.

We are at a newly developed, underground, metalliferous ore [mineral deposit containing metal] mine in 2015, and it all looks very different. In fact, the place looks more like a factory—a rock factory—than a conventional mine.

The surface works consist mainly of a series of buildings that service the main control room underground. They are so carefully landscaped into the surrounding environment that at a glance it is difficult to tell this is a mine at all.

Where Are the Miners?

But there are a couple of giveaways. One is the procession of enormous ore-filled vehicles moving between the compound and a stockpile near the processing plant. They are driverless. Another sign is the curious looking cylindrical machine that has just emerged from a three-metre diameter shaft.

At the bottom of this machine are sensors and drilling equipment to bore holes radially into the walls of the shaft. The equipment automatically sets charges that can be detonated electronically.

A siren warns of an impending blast. The earth rumbles beneath our feet as a series of muffled explosions occur in quick succession, each one shallower than the last. Within 20 minutes a robotic vehicle emerges with the first load of newly broken ore for processing.

The miners themselves are away from the equipment and the mining faces in an air-conditioned control room. And the mine they are operating is mimicked on a computer screen.

The blast has created an annular [circular] column or broken rock around the shaft. It is funneled into remote-controlled vehicles at the bottom.

After preliminary crushing, the ore is brought to the surface up a spiral roadway by truck. All this is done automatically. The only people who regularly venture into the mine are the members of the service crews for maintenance, planning and inspection.

Autonomous Mining

The above is a description of the Remote Ore Extraction System (ROES) now under development by a team led by Jock Cunningham at CSIRO Exploration & Mining. It integrates several technologies that have already been developed—autonomous underground vehicles, navigation and guidance technology, advanced radio communications, and advanced control hardware and software.

ROES is projected to reduce mining costs because it removes the need for elaborate infrastructure to gain access to ore and to support miners underground.

"We are taking a fresh look at the whole mining concept, and developing equipment designed for computers to undertake the fine control, not people," Mr. Cunningham says.

Fewer People, More Safety

The automated system will improve mine safety by removing people from hazardous environments underground, and it should open up lower-grade deposits and those that are difficult to mine.

By 2015, the advanced mine will also be using new techniques and materials for automated hard rock cutting to build access roads and tap into narrower veins of ore. And specially

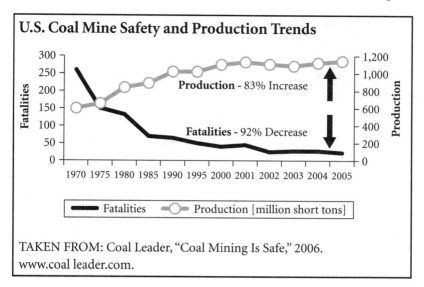

U.S. Coal Mine Safety and Production Trends

Production - 83% Increase

Fatalities - 92% Decrease

1970 1975 1980 1985 1990 1995 2000 2001 2002 2003 2004 2005

Fatalities — Production [million short tons]

TAKEN FROM: Coal Leader, "Coal Mining Is Safe," 2006. www.coal leader.com.

developed sensors should enable the new cutters to follow seams of ore automatically.

All these advances depend upon technologies that are being developed by CSIRO and its collaborators. This is not an unrealistic science fiction future but, according to Jock Cunningham, one that is already achievable given our present state of knowledge.

But it is only one scenario. Whether people are engineered out of the equipment used for mining will depend on how the industry develops structurally and financially.

Laser Scanned Mines

Right now, at WMC [Resource's] Olympic Dam mine in South Australia and [mining company] Rio Tinto's Northparkes mine in New South Wales, ore is being moved around underground by load haul dump (LHD) vehicles which are driverless and navigate themselves.

These autonomous underground vehicles travel the mine passages with minimal human involvement by using laser-scanning technology to recognise natural features.

The system, which can be retrofitted to existing vehicles, is a result of research undertaken by CSIRO and Dynamic Automation Systems (DAS) with support from the mining industry through the Australian Mineral Industries Research Association and CRC Mining.

It is now being commercialised by DAS in collaboration with CSIRO and several Australian high-tech companies.

Sensing, Imaging Software: The New Mining

This is the present frontline of mine automation in Australia. It brings together several of the technologies necessary to proceed further—sensing and imaging, wireless communications, control software, and specially adapted heavy machinery.

Some in the mining industry think this project is the beginning of a wave of technology that will eventually remove people from hazardous mining situations above and below ground. They look towards a combination of new robotic, communications and control technologies to be integrated into a Remote Ore Extraction System (ROES) being developed at CSIRO Mining Automation.

Others, more sceptical of industry acceptance of total automation, believe that at the very least, R&D [research and development] will lead to smarter, more efficient mining technology, and safer working environments, particularly underground. John Read, Deputy Chief and Mining Science Coordinator of CSIRO Exploration & Mining, says that even if ROES is never fully adopted by the mining companies, it is important to have the vision and the dream.

Safer Mining 24/7

The important drivers towards automation are greater productivity, improved safety and concern for the environment. A report released at the end of 2001 by the Centre for International Economics estimated the direct potential payback from six CSIRO robotic mining projects (mainly to do with coal) at $4.5 billion.

Most of this payback comes in increased productivity—more consistent mining, 24 hours a day, seven days a week—but automation also removes people from unsafe or hazardous environments, saving lives and reducing injuries as Australian safety legislation is becoming less prescriptive and throwing more responsibility back on companies.

In addition to the direct human benefits, the report estimates that this safety component would contribute an economic dividend of about $150 million in reduced compensation and lost time due to injury.

The same report found that automation could open up areas of ore previously considered difficult or unsafe to exploit, worth more than $40 billion over 10 years.

The Future Envisioned

"Automation is an important plank on which to build the mine of the future," says Dr. Rob La Nauze, General Manager [of] Technology for WMC Resources. "It can help us to extract the maximum value of metal with minimum impact on the environment."

According to CSIRO Mining Automation research group leader Jock Cunningham, the greatest savings can be made by gradually introducing a system-based package of automation, in which people are removed from the places of extraction and processing to safer and more comfortable environments where they can oversee equipment at work. That way, systems can be designed to make the most efficient use of equipment without concern for protecting and supporting people.

Even if the favourable estimates above are accurate, they by no means guarantee that mining companies will be in a financial position to approve the considerable investment in new technology that automation would demand. Incremental introduction and retrofitting of many of the component technologies, however, would still benefit the industry.

Some of the problems to be solved are generic and span a range of disciplines and technologies. For example, what is the safest and most reliable form of communication underground? How can systems be made failsafe? Is it possible to develop accurate sensors to track particular minerals?

Mining Meets Exports

CSIRO, Australia's universities and cooperative research centres represent one of the few research alliances in the world with the breadth of expertise to mount a concerted attack on these sorts of problems.

Not only should this kind of R&D pay off in terms of providing technology to make the nation's mining industry competitive, but it has already spawned export services that have become more profitable than the industry itself. The recently released Action Agenda report on Mining Technology Services talks of a doubling of these exports to more than $6 billion by 2010.

> "The unwillingness to invest in proper safety mechanisms, however, and the lack of regulation enforcement have created a coal mining industry that constantly operates far beyond its safe threshold."

Economic Pressure Makes Coal Mining Unsafe

Jianjun Tu

China has dramatically increased coal production to meet demand, according to Jianjun Tu, and this is particularly hazardous for miners, as China accounts for approximately 80 percent of worldwide mining deaths. The communist government of China has initiated policies to counter dangerous mining conditions but they have mostly failed, according to the author, making coal mining in China one of the most dangerous occupations in the world. Jianjun Tu is a policy analyst and writer about China for the Jamestown Foundation.

As you read, consider the following questions:

1. What is one of the primary reasons behind China's epidemic of coal mining accidents, according to the viewpoint?

2. Why does low-cost compensation to the families of miners who have died in coal mining accidents contribute to poor safety practices, according to the viewpoint?

3. China's coal fatalities will continue in the years ahead unless certain measures are implemented, according to Jianjun Tu. What are they?

Coal extraction, by no means a safe endeavor, has had a particularly disastrous record in China [up to 2007]. According to official statistics, more than 250,000 Chinese coal miners have died in mining accidents since the inception of the People's Republic of China in 1949. In comparison, industrial nations and most of the developing world have dramatically reduced mining risks over the past decades by implementing advanced technologies and strict regulations. Therefore, while the official fatality rate per million tonnes (mt) of coal produced in China was 2.73 in 2005, it was a mere 0.04 in the United States. Even India, a sizable developing country with a notoriously poor past safety record was able to reduce this rate to less than 9% of China's current rate. With such high fatality rates, China alone accounts for approximately 80% of the total deaths in coal mine accidents worldwide. Much like its coal production statistics, the safety record of China's coal industry is full of controversy. The official coal mine fatality statistics range from 5,602 to 6,995 deaths annually in the last decade [1996–2006], though independent experts state that China's actual death toll is much higher, as mine owners routinely falsify death counts in order to avoid mine closures or fines.

Rural Deaths and a Failed Legal System

The lack of legal protection for private investments has been one of the primary factors behind China's mounting coal mine accidents. After Deng Xiaoping [former head of China's ruling Communist Party] spurred the communist country to open up its economy in 1979, China's state coal mines became encumbered by heavy welfare obligations to their bloated workforces and millions of retired workers. Unable to meet the burgeoning demand for domestic coal, Beijing [Chinese capital] was forced to allow private investment into the coal industry. In less than two decades, the share of coal production by township and village enterprises (TVE) grew from 17% in 1979 to 46% in 1997. Yet, the central government was unwilling to establish any transparent entry mechanisms or legal frameworks to protect private investment in this sector, as evidenced by Beijing's 1998 decision to close small TVE mines due to the temporary over-supply of coal caused by the Asian Financial Crisis [collapse of currencies in Thailand, South Korea, and Indonesia]. Without any long-term legal guarantees of ownership rights, private mine owners are generally unwilling to invest in the necessary safety requirements, resulting in terrible working conditions for the miners in the TVE coal mines. Unsurprisingly, TVE coal mines alone accounted for 74% of the coal mine-related fatalities in 2005, though their share of national coal production decreased to 36%.

Of the thousands of coal miners who die annually, the overwhelming majority of them are migrant peasants from rural areas, who are among the most vulnerable of the social groups in China. Unable to unionize due to the ban on independent worker unions, their monthly payments are often as low as several hundred yuan [base unit of Chinese currency]. In the 11th Five-Year Plan [a series of policy goals presented every five years by the Communist Party leadership, begun in 1953 by former Chinese leader Mao Zedong], Beijing stated that it intends to reduce the rate of coal mine fatalities by 5.5% annually, reaching 2.2 per mt [million tons] of coal produced in 2010. According to the recently revised statistics, however, China's coal production increased by 13.5% annually during the 10th Five-Year Plan (2001–2005). If the current production trend persists during the 11th Five-Year Plan,

Coal Miners Slaughter

Despite mechanization and declining fatalities in recent decades, mining (including coal, iron and other forms) is the second most perilous sector of the economy, after agriculture—with a death rate seven times that of the general work force.

The official death toll doesn't account for coal miners' greatest lurking threat, pneumoconiosis. Quietly, more than 1,000 miners and ex-miners perish each year (15,000 died during the '90s) from black lung disease. In Appalachian mining towns, it's not uncommon to see frail, discolored retirees ambling slowly, oxygen tank and breathing tube in tow.

Christopher Cook, "Coal Miners Slaughter,"
In These Times, *January 25, 2006 www.inthesetimes.com.*

Beijing's goal of reducing coal mine fatalities would actually imply an absolute increase of fatalities between 2006 and 2010.

Overcrowded Underground Mines

The reliance upon underground operations as the primary method of coal mining has had a significant impact upon the productivity as well as safety conditions of China's coal mines. In most countries throughout the world, underground mining has increasingly given way to surface operations due to the significant advantage that the latter confers upon labor productivity. For instance, the share of coal derived from surface mines in the United States has increased steadily from 25% in 1949 to 67% in 2005. As an added benefit, this structural change in the coal mining industry has led to an improved safety record. Slope failure, the principle hazard of surface mines, is much easier to control than underground mining dangers, such as roof collapses and gas explosions. Yet, both the demand and the reserves of the lower quality sub-bituminous coal [most common in the United States, mainly used in coal-fired plants] and lignite [young, soft coal with a low energy and heat content] more likely to be located in shallow coal seams, remain low in China. Higher quality bituminous [about 300 million years in age with a high-heat energy content] coal and anthracite [the hardest form of coal with a high energy potential] continue to be the industry preferences, and the private sector is unwilling to invest in the capital-intensive surface mines, leaving underground operations to dominate China's coal industry. China's reliance on labor-intensive underground operations, however, results in very low productivity—about 590 tonnes of coal per employee per year, as opposed to Australia, which posted an average of 13,297 tonnes per employee in 2005. As a result, more than 3.7 million workers are necessary for China's coal mining industry to meet the growing demand. This in and of itself contributes to the crowding of underground mines and explains why mine accidents often result in a tremendously high number of fatalities; the single gas explosion at the Sunjiawan Mine in Liaoning province on February 14, 2005, claimed the lives of 214 miners.

The Mine Is Deep and the System Corrupt

While the central government imposes increasingly stringent regulations to counter the widespread corruption in the coal mining industry, there remain places in China where "the mountains are high, and the emperor is out of sight." Mine owners commonly falsify fatality figures in mine accidents—often with substantial help from corrupt local officials—in order to avoid heavy fines and other punitive measures. For instance, when 81 miners died in Nandang County on July 17, 2001, local officials quickly teamed up with the coal mine owner to cover-up the accident. After the catastrophe was disclosed to the public, it was revealed that the head of Nandang County had received 3.21 million yuan ($410,000) in bribes during the prior two years. Similarly, in the first nine months of 2006, seven director-level officials at various Coal Mine Safety Administrations in Shanxi, China's largest coal producing province, were prosecuted for coal mine-related corruption. Given the degree of collusion between local officials and coal mine owners, the central government requires that its own State Administration of Work Safety (SAWS) directly investigate deadly coal mine accidents. The heavy work load for SAWS officials, however, inevitably limits their ability to operate at strategic and managerial levels.

The low price of compensation for the death of a miner gives mine owners little incentive to employ safety practices and mechanisms. Prior to 2004, the amount of compensation for the death of a miner in China was generally between 10,000 to 50,000 yuan ($1,300 to $6,400). The low price tag placed on human life also made it easy for owners to reach private deals with the families of the deceased miners to remain quiet, allowing for the under- and non-reporting of deaths. A significant step was taken by the Shanxi provincial government on November 30, 2005, when it became the first to increase the amount of compensation to 200,000 yuan ($25,000) per coal mine fatality, a move that in turn was adopted by other major coal producing provinces. Still, the compensation remained only a small percentage of the gross annual profit—50 million yuan ($6.4 million)—for mine owners. Given that the 2005 fatality rate in China was 2.73 miners per mt coal, the penalty imposed by the new regulation represented only 1% of the gross profit collected by mine owners. Shanxi province soon realized that the new regulation was insufficient, but rather than increase the amount of compensation required, officials instead imposed an additional fine of one million yuan ($130,000) per coal mine fatality, payable to the local government itself. The incremental penalty was counterintuitive, however, because it not only turned the widespread coal mine accidents into a lucrative source of revenue for the authorities who collected the fines but also offered significant incentives for mine owners to reach private deals with miners' families so as to avoid fines, further distorting death tolls.

Coal Consumption Runs Over Safety

Since 2000, China's coal consumption has increased at an astonishing rate of more than 10% annually. The unwillingness to invest in proper safety mechanisms, however, and the lack of regulation enforcement have created a coal mining industry that constantly operates far beyond its safe threshold. Moreover, the miscalculation of a coal surplus in late 1990s convinced Beijing to compete aggressively with other major coal exporting countries in the international market. As a result, China's coal exports grew from 17 mt in 1990 to 94 mt in 2003, further aggravating the supply and demand balance. Unsurprisingly, the combination of forcing coal output beyond the capacity of the mine, worker fatigue, safety violations and equipment failure has become a catalyst for deadly accidents. According to Zhou Xinquan, a professor at China University of Mining and Technology, China's coal mining industry under invests at least 50 billion yuan ($6.4 billion) on safety equipment.

In the six years since the SAWS was given the mandate to decrease the number of China's coal mine accidents, its policy initiatives have received only mixed reviews. Though the SAWS has imposed increasingly stringent safety regulations, it has yet to establish a consistent and transparent enforcement network across the country. Troubled by the lack of enforcement, the Energy Bureau of the National Development and Reform Commission, the regulator of China's energy sector, recently stepped in and initiated its own safety program to counter the most deadly gas explosion accidents. Although China's coal mining safety issues may eventually be addressed in the long run, coal mine accidents will continue to haunt China for years to come unless the following measures can be implemented appropriately: (1) establish transparent legal & institutional frameworks to protect the interests of all stakeholders; (2) set an aggressive quantity-based safety target; (3) hold local officials accountable; (4) allow for additional media and grassroots monitoring; and (5) eliminate incentives that seriously distort safety statistics.

> "Mining has a lower rate of injuries and illness per 100 employees than the agriculture, construction or retail trades."

Education Creates Safe Coal Mining

Susan Case

Susan Case argues in this viewpoint that coal mining is safer than its media portrayal, which usually only focuses on disasters. Case describes how West Virginia University (WVU) has a dedicated core curriculum focused on enhancing mining through research and development. WVU has a long historical legacy of training mining engineers and miners, who have gone on to long and safe careers in the mining industry. Susan Case is director of College Relations at WVU and writes for the West Virginia University Alumni Magazine.

As you read, consider the following questions:

1. In the viewpoint, chairman of the West Virginia Mining Engineering Department Syd Peng, states that coal mining is dangerous. But it is important to remember something else, according to Peng. What is it?

Susan Case, "Keeping Miners Safe: WVU at the Center of Mine Safety Initiatives," *West Virginia University Alumni Magazine*, vol. 29, Summer 2006, www.ia.wvu.edu/ ~magazine. Reproduced by permission.

2. The retirement of baby boomer miners is causing what kind of problem for the West Virginia coal industry, according to the viewpoint?

3. How is mining research funding tied to the coal market, according to the viewpoint?

In the first month of 2006, 16 West Virginia coal miners died in four separate accidents. Those dramatic and tragic events cast a national spotlight on the state's coal industry and on the topic of coal mine safety.

This is not a new concern at West Virginia University [WVU], where mining and other faculty have, over the years, conducted research in mine safety-related issues, educated mining engineers, developed training programs for rank-and-file miners, and helped shape policies to improve safety and health for coal miners.

WVU's College of Engineering and Mineral Resources is home to two departments—Mining Engineering and Mining Extension—that are involved with mine safety. The College also recently [as of 2006] sent a faculty member, Jim Dean, to Charleston [West Virginia, the State Capital] to play a key role in implementing mine safety programs for the state. Others are working to find funding for more research into mine safety issues and to apply the expertise at the University to make disasters like [the 2006] Sago [mine in West Virginia where an explosion killed twelve miners] even more of a rarity than they have already become.

Mining Engineering

The WVU Department of Mining Engineering has been educating engineers and managers for the mining industry and conducting mining-related research for more than 130 years. According to Syd Peng, department chair, the twentieth century saw remarkable improvements in safety and health for U.S. miners, and a major decline in injuries and fatalities.

"Many people still think of coal mining as a very dangerous occupation," he said, "and, certainly, as Sago reminded us, accidents do happen. But it is important to understand that coal mining in this country has become a highly regulated, high-tech industry that, in fact, has a significantly lower rate of injuries and illness than many other industries."

Safety should never be taken for granted, though, and a large percentage of the research conducted by department faculty is related to safety. For example, Peng and other faculty recently developed a Mine Roof Geology Information System for detecting fractures and estimating the rock strength for an underground mine roof. The system provides miners with real-time information and engineers with a detailed roof map depicting geological changes every five feet.

Other safety-related research undertaken recently by mining engineering faculty include the development of an integrated stability mapping system aimed at reducing injuries associated with ground falls and multiseam mining situations; a dynamic ventilation model for analyzing the movement of methane and other contaminants within a mine; the cost of coal-mine catastrophes; and an evaluation of various methods of extinguishing mine fires, among others.

Science, Math, and Safety

The department also emphasizes safety in its curriculum. With four full-time faculty members, approximately 50 undergraduates, and 20 graduate students, the program immerses students in science and math fundamentals, along with in-depth study relating to the design and safe operation of mines. Safety is integrated into every aspect of the curriculum.

But the best safety training may be the experience that students gain during paid summer internships in coal mines, an opportunity offered to every mining engineering major and taken advantage of by nearly all of them. "Even though our students are heading for careers in engineering and man-

The New Mine Workplace

Mining has a lower rate of injuries and illness per 100 employees than the agriculture, construction or retail trades. According to the Department of Labor, the accident and injury rate for miners today is comparable to that of grocery store workers.

Since 1970, coal miners have more nearly tripled their productivity, while work related injuries and fatalities have declined 45 percent and 82 percent, respectively (1970–2001).

CARE, "Advanced Technology," 2003, www.careenergy.com.

agement, getting hands-on experience working in a coal mine is very educational for them," said Peng.

Patrick Pelley, a mining engineering major, would agree. Last summer, following his freshman year at WVU, Pelley worked at [energy company] CONSOL's Enlow Fork Mine [Pennsylvania]. "I was a little nervous at first," he admits, "but everyone who worked there was friendly and helpful. I learned so much, and decided that this is a career that I will enjoy."

In today's booming coal market, mining engineers are in high demand. Most students in the department receive industry-sponsored scholarships, graduate with multiple job offers, and move quickly into management and engineering positions in the mining industry.

Training Baby Boomer Replacements

Training isn't focused only on mining engineers and managers. WVU also provides training to rank-and-file coal miners, and has been doing so for a very long time.

Since 1913, the WVU Department of Mining Extension has been working with the state's coal industry to provide training programs for coal mining jobs. With the recent growth in the coal market and the retirement of the baby boomers, the current need is very real.

"The coal industry in this state is booming [in 2006]," said Joe Spiker, interim director of mining extension, "but with the retirement of the baby boomers, there aren't enough trained miners to fill the jobs. Our mission is to provide people who want to work in the mines with the training that they need to get a job and to work safely from the outset."

The department trains more than 3,000 new and experienced coal miners each year, offering new miner classes in underground and surface mining in addition to specialized courses such as foreman/fireboss certification, EMT [emergency medical technician training] for mining certification, emergency preparedness, electrical apprentice, and others.

For many years, these classes were offered statewide in a variety of locations. The program got a permanent home last year when CONSOL Energy donated its Dolls Run facility, just west of Morgantown [West Virginia] to WVU as a permanent headquarters for the miner training program. The first class at the new facility concluded in February [2006], and every student who completed the eight-week session passed the certification exams at the end of the course.

Experienced Teaching and Hands-On Experience

"Our instructors are all experienced in coal mining, and experienced in teaching," said Spiker. "A large majority of what we cover relates to the various types of accidents that can occur, how to avoid them, and what to do if they occur. We cover all of these things in a great deal of detail. We want these miners to be as prepared as they possibly can when they go to work."

With a $3 million grant from the U.S. Department of Labor, the department is hiring additional instructors and purchasing simulators that will enable participants to gain hands-on experience with various types of mining equipment before they enter a mine. The WVU facility at Dolls Run is the northern headquarters for the training program, and Southern West Virginia Community and Technical College is coordinating the program in the southern part of the state. The West Virginia Coal Association is an important partner as well.

Leadership in Mine Safety

Joe Spiker is the interim director of mining extension because he is filling in for Jim Dean, who led the department since 1994, but was recently asked by West Virginia governor Joe Manchin to become the acting director of the West Virginia Office of Miners' Health Safety and Training—the state agency charged with enforcing state laws relating to mine safety and health.

Dean, who has bachelor's and master's degrees in mining and a high degree of expertise in mine safety and management, is now playing a key role in the state's response to the [2006] mine tragedies. His responsibilities include the implementation of new state mine safety legislation that was passed after the Sago disaster. The new legislation requires additional oxygen supplies, improved underground communications systems, and revised emergency reporting requirements for coal mine accidents.

"My goals are to provide leadership to the Office of Miners' Health Safety and Training during this difficult time," said Dean, "to focus on our agency's mission of improving mine safety through inspection and training, and to improve West Virginia's capabilities in mine rescue response."

The Coal Boom and New Mine Safety Initiatives

Thirty years ago, the last time the coal market was booming, WVU was the center of a great deal more research related to coal mine safety than it is today, said Roy Nutter, a professor of computer science and electrical engineering. Nutter and many others conducted research in underground mine communications and monitoring, ventilation systems, robots, and many other mine safety-related subjects.

"When the coal market became sluggish in the eighties, the funding for research also dried up," said Nutter. "With the market in better shape now, and the current interest in mine safety, we hope that there will be more funding for research in these areas. Our faculty offers a great deal of expertise, and we're eager to help."

Dick Bajura, director of WVU's National Research Center for Coal and Energy (NRCCE), seconds that opinion.

"There is little doubt," said Bajura, "that the federal government needs to pay more attention to health and safety issues relating to coal mining, that more funding is needed for research in these areas. [West Virginia] Senator [Robert] Byrd is pushing for this to happen, and I am confident that it will."

The NRCCE is also working on mine safety initiatives at the state level. The agency recently hosted a West Virginia Mine Safety Roundtable that brought together representatives from government, industry, labor, academia, and other groups to discuss challenges and opportunities presented by West Virginia's new mine safety legislation.

"We hope to continue to support the efforts of all of those who are working for the improvement of our state's coal mining industry," said Bajura.

> *"If the sorry history of the coal mining industry has proven one thing, it's that when it comes to enacting and enforcing safety laws against Big Coal, the only good lobbyists are dead miners."*

Coal Mining Satety Cannot Be Taught

Jeff Goodell

Jeff Goodell argues in this viewpoint that the coal industry seeks to portray modern mining as safe and efficient. Goodell claims this is nonsense, offering arguments that reveal how dangerous and exploitive coal mining is to the workers engaged in it. Jeff Goodell is a contributing editor at Rolling Stone *and author of* Our Story, *an account of nine miners trapped underground after the Quecreek, Pennsylvania, mine collapse in 2002.*

As you read, consider the following questions:

1. The coal industry, according to Goodall, suggests that the average miner earns approximately fifty thousand dollars a year. Is this accurate, according to the viewpoint?

2. The Jim Walters Resources No. 5 mine in Alabama collapsed on September 23, 2001, killing thirteen coal miners. According to Goodall, what was the U.S. Mining Safety and Health Agency's (MISHA) relationship to the mine at the time of the accident?

3. West Virginia senator Robert Byrd gave a speech on the Senate floor after the Sago mine disaster in 2006. What, according to the viewpoint, was the substance of his speech, as it related to coalmining?

Big Coal works overtime to suggest that coal mining today has nothing in common with its dark and exploitative past. The old days of breaker boys and methane explosions and black lung are gone, the coal industry argues, and mining today is safe, well paid, and professional. Images of coal miners in promotional literature published by the National Mining Association and others always show clean-faced men in close proximity to high-tech machinery—computer screens, Global Positioning System (GPS) equipment, bright yellow haul trucks. The average salary of a coal miner, the association boasts, is $50,000 a year. According to one coal industry Web site, working in a coal mine today is as safe as working in a grocery store.

Of course, that is nonsense. Working in a coal mine in West Virginia may be much safer than working in a coal mine in China, but according to the National Institute for Occupational Safety and Health, mining is still one of the most dangerous occupations in America. Working in an underground coal mine, especially one owned by a small, non-union operator, such as Quecreek, is most dangerous of all. The fatality rate in these mines is five times higher than it is in surface coal mines. Although mining fatalities fell precipitously after the passage of the Federal Coal Mine Health and Safety Act in 1969, the numbers have leveled off since then. Many of the deaths in recent years could have been prevented. In one case, after thirteen men were killed in a methane explosion in an

Alabama coal mine in 2001, investigations indicated that the mine openly flouted basic safety regulations. Similarly, after the Sago mine exploded in West Virginia in 2006, it was discovered that the mine had been cited for more than two hundred federal safety violations during the previous year. And despite the coal industry's claims that black lung is a disease of the past, more than 1,500 (mostly retired) miners still die from it every year.

Claims about the high wages earned by today's coal miners are also distorted. Like most blue-collar workers, coal miners have not shared in the bounty of economic progress during the past several decades. According to U.S. Department of Labor statistics, the average weekly wage of a coal miner in 2004 was about 20 percent lower than it was in 1985 (adjusted for inflation), despite the fact that the average miner's per-shift productivity had nearly tripled in the same period. Wages vary widely from mine to mine. In the East, union mines pay 20 to 30 percent more than non-union, and nationwide strip mines, generally pay better than underground mines. A heavy equipment operator at a big strip mine in the West can make $60,000 a year or more. By contrast, an underground laborer in a mine like Quecreek, where the risk of injury and death is far higher, makes only half that. Although coal jobs are often touted as work that can't be outsourced to China, the industry has consistently threatened to shut down mines and cut back operations in order to force workers to agree to wage and benefit cuts. Thanks to aggressive union busters like Don Blankenship [CEO of Massey Energy Corporation, one of the largest coal mining businesses in West Virginia], as well as years of misguided union leadership, union mines in the East have been hardest hit. The United Mine Workers of America, once one of the most powerful voices for workers in the country, has seen its membership decimated in recent decades. Today the union represents only about 40 percent of U.S. mineworkers, and the percentage is falling every year....

Coal Mining, De-Unionized and Deregulated

With far less public notice and comment by policy-makers, the same process of replacement of union by non-union work, which is threatening the U.S. auto and auto parts industries, has hit the nation's coal mines since the 1990s—especially during the reign of "Energy Task Force Cheney [2001 energy task force led by vice president Dick Cheney to develop a U.S energy policy]." In the country's new strip-mining center, the Powder River Basin of Cheney's Wyoming and Montana, the mine workforce—largely never unionized—has paid with the lack of health care and pension benefits, and often with lower wages. But in the older, largely deep-mining Appalachian center from West Virginia and Kentucky down to Alabama—where "distressed" mines are being acquired and stripped of their unions along with their coal—miners are paying with their lives.

The forcing process since 2002, is one of deregulation, and mergers and acquisitions by very large international coal speculators and banks, during which the mine-mouth price of a ton of coal for electric generation has doubled to $30–35. The resulting drive to double and triple production from old, heavily worked mines is playing havoc with safety regulations, and killing miners. After much boasting by the deregulators that "self-regulation" caused there to be only 22 mine deaths nationally in 2005, January 2006 alone has seen 19 miners die, 16 of them in West Virginia's mines.

Paul Gallagher and Mark Bender, "West Virginia Coal Crisis: A Matter of Criminal Negligence?" Executive Intelligence Review, *February 10, 2006, http://larouchepub.com.*

If the sorry history of the coal mining industry has proven one thing, it's that when it comes to enacting and enforcing safety laws against Big Coal, the only good lobbyists are dead miners. Even the public outrage that followed the disaster in Monongah [West Virginia] in 1907, which left 250 widows and 1,000 fatherless kids, was not enough to push Congress to pass safety laws against the all-powerful coal industry. It took another dozen mine disasters throughout the country, and another 1,200 or so dead miners, before Congress finally acted, creating the U.S. Bureau of Mines in the Department of the Interior in 1910, with instructions to investigate mining methods, "especially with respect to miners, and . . . the possible improvements of conditions under which mining operations are carried on." But the legislation provided no enforcement power whatsoever, and investigators could enter a mine only with the permission of the owner and were not allowed to publicize their findings. It took another three decades—and many thousands of dead coal miners—before Congress granted the bureau the authority to inspect mines and publicize its findings. But it still had no enforcement power.

In 1947, an explosion in a mine in Centralia, Illinois, killed 111 miners. An investigation later revealed that years of warnings about dangerous conditions in the mine were contemptuously ignored by the mine owner. Testifying before Congress, John L. Lewis, the powerful head of the United Mine Workers of America, thundered, "If we must grind up human flesh and bone in the industrial machine we call modern America, then before God I assert that those who consume coal and you and I who benefit from that service because we live in comfort, we owe protection to those men first, and we owe security to their families if they die." In 1952, President Harry Truman—one of the few U.S. presidents who had the courage to stand up to Big Coal—signed the Federal Coal Mine Safety Act. The legislation was full of loopholes, written into the law by coal industry lobbyists, but for the first time, it gave mine inspectors the power to shut down certain types of dangerous mines.

It still didn't stop the deaths. In 1968, an explosion in Consolidation Coal's No. 9 mine in Farmington, West Virginia, killed seventy-eight miners. The mine had had a history of accidents. It had blown up in 1954, killing sixteen men, and in the two years before the 1968 explosion, inspectors had cited Consolidated Coal for numerous safety violations. The mine was destroyed by the 1968 blast and burned for several days. To smother the flames, the mine was sealed shut, and the bodies of the miners were never recovered. Once again, there were calls for the government to crack down on Big Coal. "Let me assure you," Secretary of the Interior Stewart Udall told a conference on mine safety, "the people of this country will no longer accept the disgraceful health and safety record that has characterized this major industry." The following year, Congress passed the Federal Coal Mine Health and Safety Act, which dramatically increased the enforcement powers of the Bureau of Mines. It also gave miners the right to request a federal inspection and, for the first time, provided benefits to miners disabled by black lung. It was landmark legislation, but it had come too late for the nearly 100,000 coal miners who had already been killed since 1900.

In the years after the bill was passed, the rate of fatal accidents declined gradually and irregularly. President Richard Nixon helped stall any tough enforcement by installing political cronies in top positions at the bureau. In 1972, the General Accounting Office reported that "the Department's policies for enforcing health and safety standards have been extremely lenient, confusing, and inequitable." In part because of this, in 1977 the power to inspect mines and enforce safety laws was transferred from the Department of the Interior to the Department of Labor, where a new agency, the Mine Safety and Health Administration (MSHA), was created. But problems of failing to enforce the law against coal companies continued. In 1987, Republican senator Orrin Hatch called MSHA "an agency in trouble," with a "disturbing pattern of misconduct, mismanagement, and serious abuse."

During the [Bill] Clinton administration, MSHA was presided over by J. Davitt McAteer, a lawyer and mine safety expert who was no friend of Big Coal. Then, in 2001, President George W. Bush restored the tradition of cronyism and lax enforcement by giving the top job at MSHA to Dave Lauriski, a former executive with Energy West Mining Company, a small underground coal producer based in Utah. Although Energy West's mines had a good safety record, Lauriski was known for his belief that the coal industry should be given increasing latitude to police itself. He had spent years lobbying MSHA to loosen the rules against dangerous levels of coal dust—the main cause of black lung—in underground mines. When Lauriski arrived at MSHA, he vowed to "make a culture change" in the agency, shifting its emphasis from enforcement to education, training, and consulting. (Mine inspectors, for example, became known as "health and safety compliance officers.") As if that weren't enough, Lauriski's boss, Secretary of Labor Elaine Chao, was the wife of Kentucky Republican senator Mitch McConnell, one of Big Coal's staunchest supporters. And no wonder: according to Common Cause from 1997 to 2000, the coal industry gave $584,000 to the National Republican Senatorial Committee, the soft-money machine that McConnell then chaired. Despite his insistence that there was no conflict of interest, McConnell left his fingerprints all over his wife's agency. Chao even hired several of McConnell's Senate staffers to work in top positions at the Department of Labor, including Chao's chief of staff, Steven Law, who had been one of McConnell's top aides.

Coal operators were not bashful about exploiting these political connections. In 2002, notoriously outspoken Ohio mine owner Bob Murray threatened to have some MSHA inspectors fired because they had cited his mines for failing to comply with regulations. "Mitch McConnell calls me one of the five finest men in America," Murray told the inspectors, according to local press accounts. "And the last time I checked, he was sleeping with your boss."

It wasn't long before tragedy struck again. On September 23, 2001, as many Americans watched the World Trade Center memorial service at [New York's] Yankee Stadium, a crew of thirty-two miners descended into the deepest coal mine in North America, near Brookwood, Alabama. The Jim Walter Resources No. 5 mine was twice as deep as the World Trade Center had been high, and it was one of the most hazardous mines in the country, with a long history of safety violations, many of which related to the buildup of dangerous methane gas. At about 5:15 P.M., a fifty-six-year-old miner named Gaston Adams Jr. and three others were working to shore up an unstable roof. When part of the roof collapsed, a falling rock hit a sofasize battery charger, sparking a methane explosion. When the dust cleared, Adams was pinned beneath the debris. He gave his head-lamp to his buddies and told them to get out. But when news spread that Adams was trapped, twelve of his fellow miners decided that instead of evacuating, they would try to save him. It was a heroic, but fatal, decision. Forty-five minutes later, a second, more powerful blast killed them all and set off a fire that raged for three days, until the company flooded the shaft. It was the worst coal mining disaster in nearly twenty years, and yet because it happened just twelve days after 9/11, most Americans never heard of it.

After investigating the explosion in the mine, which was non-union, the United Mine Workers accused MSHA of treating "serious violations such as . . . disruptions in the mine's ventilation system" as "minor infractions." The union claimed that MSHA did not respond to "requests by the miners for increased inspections when serious hazards existed," that the agency provided the mine owner with advance notice of inspection locations, and that an "MSHA supervisor divert an inspector away from an area of the mine that had known ventilation problems just prior to the explosion." At the time of the disaster, the mine had thirty-one outstanding violations, and federal inspectors had not bothered to determine whether they had been corrected. Just six days before the explosion, MSHA inspectors wrote that methane concentrations posed an "imminent danger." Why was nothing done? One surviving miner, Robert Tarvin, pointed to the cozy relationship between MSHA and Jim Walter Resources: one of the MSHA officials to whom mine inspectors reported had recently been a manager at Walter Resources. "Going out for dinner and playing golf and this junk," Tarvin said with a scowl.

"If you know the history of this industry," observed Joe Main, the health and safety director for the United Mine Workers, "you can see why miners would be concerned when coal company bosses take over the administration of mine safety and health laws."

After the explosion in the Sago mine in 2006, questions were again raised about MSHA's competency and its willingness to enforce mining laws. "Where is MSHA?" West Virginia Senator Robert Byrd asked during a fiery Senate floor speech not long after the bodies of the twelve men were pulled from the mine. "What is that agency waiting for?" Byrd complained that the Sago mine had received 276 MSHA citations over the last two years [2004–2006] but was still allowed to operate. "Could an automobile driver or a truck driver rack up 276 speeding tickets and still have a license? What if someone had 276 mistakes on a tax return?" Byrd asked. "But here was a coal company with 276 violations and still operating."

In the aftermath of the tragedy, Congressman George Miller, the ranking Democrat on the committee that oversees MSHA, called on the Bush administration to dramatically increase fines against mining companies that repeatedly violate federal safety rules. In a letter to Labor Secretary Chao, Miller pointed out that MSHA fined the owners of the Sago mine just $24,374 for the citations issued in 2005, or an average of only $156 per violation. Many of these citations, Miller noted, "were the result of repeated violations of the same rules and regulations, over and over." For example, one citation in December 2005 for accumulation of combustible material received a $60 fine. It was the twenty-first citation that year for the same type of violation. "In such a profitable industry, there is no reason to tolerate repeat violations by mine operators," Miller wrote in his letter to Chao. "When a speeding ticket in West Virginia costs more than the twenty-first citation for accumulation of combustible materials, there is something horribly wrong with mine safety enforcement."

Periodical Bibliography

The following articles have been selected to supplement the diverse views presented in this chapter.

China Through a Lens	"Li Yizhong's War on Recurring Coal Mine Accidents," August 2006, www.china.org.cn.
Simon Elegant	"Where the Coal Is Stained with Blood," *Time*, March 12, 2007, www.time.com.
Stuart Elliot	"They're Looking for a Few Good Coal Miners," *New York Times*, March 23, 2007, www.nytimes.com.
Environmental News Service	"Federal Judge Rules Mountaintop Removal Coal Mining Illegal," March 24, 2007, www.ens-newswire.com.
Jeff Goodell	"You Fight for What You've Got, Even If It's Only Worth a Dime," *O, The Oprah Magazine*, July 2006, www.oprah.com.
Maria Guzzo	"Safety to Impact Coal Mines but Extent Unclear," *American Metal Market*, March 21, 2006, www.amm.com.
Brian Salgado	"Safety Is Still No. 1: As United Coal Co. Returns to the Mining Industry after a Seven-Year Absence, Safety Remains Top Priority at its Mines," *Exploration and Processing*, Summer 2006, www.exploration-processing.com.
James Sharpe	"All Mining Is Coal Mining (Safety of People Under Coal Mines)," *Rock Products*, November 1, 2006, www.rockproducts.com.
Steve Twedt	"Coal Group, Feds at Odds Over Emergency Oxygen," *Pittsburgh Post-Gazette*, April 10, 2007, www.post-gazette.com.
Ken Ward Jr.	"Shafted: How the Bush Administration Reversed Decades of Progress on Mine Safety," *Washington Monthly*, March 2007, www.washingtonmonthly.com.

For Further Discussion

Chapter 1

1. U.S. Department of Energy, which provided the study report on the future of coal, and Travis Madsen and Rob Sargent agree that the world is experiencing a "coal rush," as both developing and nondeveloping countries seek alternatives to oil and natural gas. In the opinion of either set of authors, does a replacement alternative to coal exist as of 2007? How does the speed of technological development relate to the speed of climate change, in the opinions of both pairs of authors?

2. "Energy security" is a term that several authors in chapter 1 use. What does it mean? Why do authors arguing for and against coal as the energy future see it as a key concept?

3. S.C. Gwynne argues that there are no easy answers to future energy needs in Texas. Former Greenpeace founder Patrick Moore believes that nuclear power, which he once opposed, now might be an answer to U.S. fossil fuel dependence. Based on his viewpoint argument, would Moore be able to convince Gwynne that nuclear power could help Texas meet its future energy needs?

Chapter 2

1. Michael Shedlock, in the chapter's opening viewpoint, argues for coal's justifiable use based on a financial investor's global perspective. Tim Folger argues in the third viewpoint that coal is a viable, long-term energy source if it can be made to burn cleaner. Could both authors agree that coal has a justifiable place in the energy future? Under what terms could they agree? Do any of the

viewpoints that follow theirs offer an alternative that both might agree justifies coal use?

2. Why does the Navajo Nation, in viewpoint four, allow coal mining on its reservation but not uranium mining? In the opinion of the viewpoint author, James Finch, is the economics of mining always based on sound science?

3. Former U.S. Department of Energy secretary Spencer Abraham argues in chapter 2 that collaborations between coal-using, industrial nations will further technological changes, making coal environmentally friendly. Do the technological advances Abraham envisions help the labor side of the coal mining process? How would Robin Nieto's viewpoint about coal mining in Venezuela answer that question?

Chapter 3

1. The Irish government banned the use of residential bituminous coal in certain urban regions of Ireland because, in its opinion, coal use caused more air pollution than industrial coal burning. Would it be possible to ban industrial coal burning within a decade, according to the other viewpoints in the chapter? If so, what would you think would be the consequences? If not, how might the Irish ban shape the decision to allow coal burning to continue?

2. The World Coal Institute argues that coal cannot be banned because it is too vital to the world's economy. Mark Hertsgaard argues that one of the major funders of coal plants in the developing world, the World Bank, should ban financing of coal-fired generators. Could the ideas that the World Coal Institute promotes still be achieved even if the World Bank decided to halt coal fuel funding? Does your answer help explain whose original argument is more persuasive?

Chapter 4

1. Jeff Goodell and Samuel Davidson seem to agree in their viewpoints that mine safety failures have led to coal miner deaths. Do they both believe that more government regulation of the mining industry would prevent fatalities?

2. Tim Thwaites presents a virtual, zero-accident mine of the future in his viewpoint. Jianjun Tu describes antiquated Chinese coal mining, an industry that leads the world in mining accidents and death. Thwaites argues for a future in which coal mining does not require many, if any, coal miners. Based on Jianjun Tu's viewpoint, do you think China would ever allow its industry to be transformed along the lines Thwaites describes? Why or why not?

3. Susan Case argues for college education of mining industry personnel in her viewpoint. Jeff Goodell argues against an industry he feels is a corporate machine that has little regard for the safety of coal miners. Based on the two viewpoints, do you think that colleges, such as West Virginia University, can act as a mediating safety adviser to miners and the industry? Could such a scenario help improve the safety record in mining?

Organizations to Contact

The editors have compiled the following list of organizations concerned with the issues debated in this book. The descriptions are derived from materials provided by the organizations. All have publications or information available for interested readers. The list was compiled on the date of publication of the present volume; the information provided here may change. Be aware that many organizations take several weeks or longer to respond to inquiries, so allow as much time as possible.

American Coal Ash Association (ACAA)
15200 East Girard Ave., Suite 3050, Aurora, CO 80014
(720) 870-7897
e-mail: info@acaa-usa.org
Web site: www.acaa-usa.org

The American Coal Ash Association is a nonprofit organization that promotes reuse of coal combustion products (CCPs), the residue left over from burning coal in a boiler. CCPs can substitute for natural or manufactured materials in a variety of commercial applications and products. ACAA publishes *Ash at Work Magazine*, containing a variety of articles on CCPs, which can be downloaded from the Web site.

American Coal Council (ACC)
2980 E. Northern Ave., Suite B5, Phoenix, AZ 85028
(602) 485-4737 • fax: (602) 485-4847
e-mail: info@americancoalcouncil.org
Web site: www.americancoalcouncil.org

The American Coal Council is a private trade industry group organized to promote development and use of American coal to enhance economic and energy security through an environmentally sound policy. The ACC promotes a nonadversarial approach to partnering coal businesses that mine, sell, trade, transport, market, or use coal, providing educational and technical support in a peer-to-peer atmosphere. The Council publishes *American Coal Magazine* and the *American Coal Advisory Newsletter*, along with fact sheets and industry case studies.

American Coal Foundation (ACF)
101 Constitution Ave., NW, Washington, DC   20001-2133
(202) 463-9785 • fax: (202) 463-9786
e-mail: info@teachcoal.org
Web site: www.teachcoal.org

The American Coal Foundation is a nonprofit, nonlobbying organization designed to develop, produce, and circulate coal-related educational information and programs designed for students and teachers. The ACF has been supported at various times by coal producers, mining suppliers and equipment manufacturers, electric utilities, railroads, and unions. The Foundation's Web site contains articles such as *Coal's Past, Present, and Future*, and activity booklets such as *Let's Learn About Coal* and *Power from Coal*.

American Geological Institute (AGI)
4220 King St., Alexandria, VA   22302-1502
(703) 379-2480 • fax: (702) 379-7563
e-mail: agi@agiweb.org
Web site: www.agiweb.org

AGI is a nonprofit organization dedicated to serving the geoscience community of geologists, geophysicists, and earth and environmental scientists. It provides outreach and educational services, while striving to help the general public understand the crucial role geosciences play in the use of earth resources and its interaction with the environment. Publications include short books such as *Coal and the Environment*.

Citizens Coal Council (CCC)
670 Jefferson Ave., Washington, PA   15301
(724) 222-5602 • fax: (724) 222-5609
Web site: www.citizenscoalcouncil.org

Citizens Coal Council is comprised of twenty-eight environmental grassroots groups and individuals working to promote ecological and social justice. Their aim is to protect people, homes, communities, land, and water from coal industry operations and to enforce the Surface Mining Control and Reclamation Act, the law coal companies are meant to adhere to during and after mining operations. The CCC Web site contains articles such as "Analysis of President Bush's National Energy Policy for Coal and Its Impact on the Environment" and "Mountaintop Removal Strip Mining."

Greenpeace
702 H St., NW, Washington, DC   20001
(202) 462-1177
e-mail: info@wdc.greenpeace.org
Web site: www.greenpeace.org

An international organization dedicated to environmental protection, Greenpeace uses peaceful direct action and creative communication strategies to inform the worldwide public on a variety of subjects, for example, on the dangers of animal extinction and global warming. Greenpeace is supported only by direct donations from individuals worldwide. Its Web site contains a variety of articles on environmental action, research, and resources, including "America Can Solve Global Warming Without Nukes, Without Continued Dependence on Coal."

Intergovernmental Panel on Climate Control
IPCC Secretariat, Geneva 2, CH-1211   C.P. 2300
   Switzerland
e-mail: IPCC-Sec@wmo.int
Web site: www.ipcc.ch

IPCC is a collaborative organization made up of the World Meteorological Organization (WMO) and the United Nations Environment Program (UNEP), created to objectively assess and understand scientific and technical information relating to global climate change and its potential impact on the Earth.

IPCC's Web site contains data profiles, press releases and speeches, and reports, including "Special Report on Carbon Dioxide Capture and Storage."

International Energy Agency (IEA) Clean Coal Centre
Gemini House, London, U.K. SWl5 6AA
+44 (0)20 8780 2111 • fax: +44 (0)20 8780 1746
e-mail: mail@iea-coal.org.uk
Web site: www.iea-coal.org.uk

The IEA Clean Coal Centre provides data and publications on sustainable coal use worldwide to governments and the coal industry through analysis, advice, and technical assistance. The center maintains databases on coal information and technologies. Reports available on the IEA Clean Coal Centre's Web site include "Summary of Canadian Clean Power Coalition Work on CO^2 Storage and Capture," and "The Impact of Emissions Trading on the Coal Industry."

International Energy Initiative (IEI)
Gilberto de Martino Jannuzzi, Campinas, SP   13083-970
    Brazil
+55 19 3788 3282 • fax: +55 19 2038/3722
e-mail: jannuzzi@fem.unicamp.br
Web site: www.ieiglobal.org

The International Energy Initiative is a nonprofit organization dedicated to providing balanced analysis of sustainable energies, including renewable, high-efficiency systems, and hardware and software that advances the goal of sustainability. The organization seeks to advise developing countries on their energy goals and policies. IEI publishes the *Energy for Sustainable Development Journal*, which includes articles such as "Towards a Policy Model for Climate Change Mitigation: China's Experience with Wind Power Development and Lessons for Developing Countries," and "Climate Change Mitigation and Sustainable Development Through Carbon Sequestration: Experiences in Latin America."

Kentucky Coal Association (KCA)
340 S. Broadway, Suite 100, Lexington, KY   40508-2553
(859) 233-4743 • fax: (859) 233-4745
e-mail: kca@kentuckycoal.com
Web site: www.kentuckycoal.org

The Kentucky Coal Association is a nonprofit organization dedicated to helping union and nonunion surface and underground miners and industry companies reach consensual agreement on and solve the most pressing problems of the coal mining industry. Its Web site contains Kentucky coal mining history and editorial articles published in Kentucky newspapers such as "Mining Is Safer than Most Realize," and "Mountaintop Mining Critics Ignore Reclamation."

National Mining Association (NMA)
101 Constitution Ave., NW, Washington, DC   20001-2133
(202) 463-2600 • fax: (202) 463-2666
e-mail: craulston@nma.org
Web site: www.nma.org

The National Mining Association is a nonprofit trade association and mining advocacy organization composed of lobbyists, lawyers, and regulatory experts who consult with the mining industry to develop and promote mining industry policy. NMA publishes *NMA Mining Week,* which contains articles such as "Supreme Court Rules Clean Air Act Covers Carbon Dioxide Emissions" and "GAO Report Identifies CTL (coal to liquid) Fuels as Key Component of Federal Energy Security Plan."

Renewable Energy Policy Project (REPP)
1612 K St. NW, Suite 202, Washington, DC   20006
(202) 293-2898 • fax: (202) 293-5857
e-mail: info2@repp.org
Web site: www.crest.org

The goal of the Renewable Energy Policy Project is to accelerate the expansion of renewable energy by offering analysis-basis, credible information, and strategies to transform energy markets. The organization researches energy issues and their relation to emergent environmental concerns, offering policy tools to help people negotiate and understand new renewable energy markets. REEP's Web site hosts onine renewable energy discussion groups and offers publications that can be downloaded, such as "Powering the South: A Clean and Affordable Energy Plan for the Southern United States."

U.S. Department of Energy (DOE)
1000 Independence Ave., SW, Washington, DC   20585
800-342-5363 • fax: (202) 586-4403
e-mail: The.Secretary@hq.doe.gov
Web site: www.energy.gov

The U.S. Department of Energy is charged with fostering a safe and reliable energy system that is environmentally and economically sustainable and to support scientific leadership in developing innovative energy technologies and strategies. The DOE Web site contains a link to its Office of Science education program, containing "Ask a Scientist," where high school students can forward energy science questions on topics not commonly found in textbooks and search the archive of previously asked questions from their contemporaries (www.newton.dep.anl.gov/aas.htm). The DOE Web site also includes *Quarterly Coal Report* and various coal publications.

U.S. Department of Labor
Mine Safety and Health Administration (MSHA)
Arlington, VA   22209-3939
(202) 693-9400 • fax: (202) 693-9401
e-mail: zzMSHA-asmsha@dol.gov
Web site: www.msha.gov

The Mine Safety and Health Administration is responsible for mine inspections, promoting regulatory compliance with mining laws, and providing health and safety technical assistance and training to management and workers in the mining industry. The MSHA Web site contains numerous articles and updates on the state of mining in the United State, including "Darby Mine No. 1, Fatal Underground Coal Mine Explosion," and "Breathable Air: Questions and Answers."

United Mountain Defense (UMD)

PO Box 20363, Knoxville, TN   37920
(865) 633-8483
e-mail: unitedmountaindefense@yahoo.com
Web site: www.unitedmountaindefense.org

United Mountain Defense is a nonprofit organization dedicated to stopping the use of mountaintop coal removal processes in Tennessee and thereby protecting the state's natural environment. UMD conducts scientific monitoring, data collection, public education, and legal and policy advocacy. The UMD Web site contains descriptions of and data derived from mountaintop coal removal and articles such as "Economics of Strip Mining" and "Site Visit to the Three Mines Proposed for the Egan Area of Claiborne County."

Bibliography of Books

Matthew Allen   *Undermining the Japanese Miracle: Work and Conflict in a Japanese Coalmining Community*. Cambridge: Cambridge University, 1994.

Huw Beyon, et al.   *Digging Up Trouble: The Environmental Protest and Opencast Mining*. London: Rivers Oram, 2000.

David P. Bridges   *The Best Coal Company in All Chicago, and How It Got That Way*. Melbourne, Australia: Bookman, 2003.

Albert Dean Browning   *Death, Destruction, and Disaster in the American Coal Mining Industry (2001)*. Bloomington, IN: Authorhouse, 2003.

Peter Crow   *Do, Die, or Get Along: A Tale of Two Appalachian Towns*. Athens: University of Georgia, 2007.

C.F. Eble, D.C. Peters, A.R. Papp, S.F. Greb   *Coal and the Environment*. Alexandria, VA: American Geological Institute, 2006.

Barbara Freese   *Coal: A Human History*. Cambridge MA: Perseus, 2003.

Ross Gelbspan   *Boiling Point: How Politicians, Big Oil and Coal, Journalists and Activists Are Fueling the Climate Crisis—and What We Can Do to Avert Disaster*. New York: Basic, 2004.

Martha Hostetter, ed.	*Energy Policy.* New York: H.W. Wilson, 2002.
F.W. Kindermann, ed.	*Coal Winning.* New York: Routledge, 2004.
Elizabeth Kolbert	*Field Notes from a Catastrophe: Man, Nature, and Climate Change.* New York: Bloomsbury USA, 2006.
K.A. Sear Lindon, ed.	*The Properties and Use of Coal Fly Ash: A Valuable Industrial By-Product.* London: Thomas Telford, 2006.
Scott Martelle	*Blood Passions: The Ludlow Massacre and Class War in the American West.* New Brunswick, NJ: Rutgers University Press, 2007.
Gary McGaughey	*Assessing the Air Quality Impacts Associated with the Proposed Construction of Fifteen New Coal-Fired Power Plants in Texas.* Austin: University of Texas, 2007.
Arthur McIvor and Ronald Johnston	*Miners' Lung: A History of Dust Disease in British Coal Mining.* Aldershot, U.K.: Ashgate, 2007.
Andrew McKillop and Shelia Newman, eds.	*The Final Energy Crisis.* Ann Arbor, MI: Pluto, 2005.
Ewan McLeish	*Energy Crisis.* North Mankato, MN: Stargazer, 2007.
Donald L. Miller and R.E. Sharpless	*Kingdom of Coal.* Philadelphia: University of Pennsylvania, 1986.

Stephen J. Mills   *Prospects for Coal and Clean Coal Technologies in Poland.* London: IEA Clean Coal Centre, 2007.

Chad Montrie   *To Save the Land and People: A History of Opposition to Surface Coal Mining in Appalachia.* Chapel Hill: University of North Carolina, 2002.

Friederike Most   *Coal Mine: Work in the Mine.* Zurich: Edition Stemmle, 1998.

Alena Mudroch,   *Remediation of Abandoned Surface*
et al., eds.   *Coal Mining Sites.* New York: Springer 2002.

National Resource   *Coal Waste Impoundments: Risks, Re-*
Council   *sponses, and Alternatives.* Washington, DC: National Academy, 2002.

Roy L. Nersesian   *Energy for the 21st Century: A Comprehensive Guide to Conventional and Alternative Sources.* Armonk, NY: M.E. Sharpe, 2007.

Joan Quigley   *The Day the Earth Caved In: An American Mining Tragedy.* New York: Random House, 2007.

Erik Reece   *Lost Mountain: A Year in the Vanishing Wilderness: Radical Strip Mining and the Devastation of Appalachia.* New York: Riverhead, 2006.

Dohn Riley and   *Turning the Corner: Energy Solutions*
Mark McLaughlin   *for the 21st Century.* Canyon, TX: Alternative Energy Institute, 2001.

David Robertson

Hard as the Rock Itself: Place and Identity in the American Mining Town. Boulder: University of Colorado, 2006.

Dan Rottenberg

In the Kingdom of Coal: An American Family and the Rock that Changed the World. New York: Routledge, 2003.

Andrew Roy

A History of the Coal Miners of the United States. Ithaca, NY: Cornell University, 2007.

Alex Schust

Gary Hollow: A History of the Largest Coal Mining Operation in the World. Charleston, WV: Two Mule, 2005.

Daniel Sperling and James S. Cannon, eds.

The Hydrogen Energy Transition: Moving Toward the Post-Petroleum Age in Transportation. London: Elsevier, 2004.

D.J. Swaine and F. Goodarzi, eds.

Environmental Aspects of Trace Elements in Coal. Dordecht, Netherlands: Kluwer Academic, 2006.

Larry Thomas

Coal Geology. Chichester, West Sussex, UK: Wiley, 2002.

Elspeth Thomson

Chinese Coal Industry—An Economic History. London: Routledge-Curzon, 2002.

U.S. House of Representatives — *Future of Federal Coal: Status, Availability, and Impact of Technological Advances in Using Coal to Create Alternative Energy Resources.* Subcommittee on Energy and Mineral Resources of the Committee on Resources. Washington, DC: United States Government Printing Office, 2006.

A. Williams, M. Pourkashanian, J.M. Jones, et al. — *Combustion and Gasification of Coal.* New York: Taylor and Francis, 2000.

Index